Your New Dog

ALSO BY SUSAN McCULLOUGH

Housetraining for Dummies
  (Hungry Minds, 2002)

New Choices in Natural Healing for Dogs and Cats
  (Rodale Press, 1999)—contributor

The Well-Mannered Dog
  (Rodale Press, 1999)—contributor

PetSpeak
  (Rodale Press, 2000)—contributor

Chicken Soup for the Cat and Dog Lover's Soul
  (Health Communications, 1999)—contributor

A **Pets Are Family Too** Book

Your New Dog

An Expert Answers Your Every Question

SUSAN McCULLOUGH

CAPITAL BOOKS, INC. • STERLING, VIRGINIA

Talia Greenberg, illustrator.
Design and composition by Melissa Ehn at Wilsted & Taylor Publishing Services.

Library of Congress Cataloging-in-Publication Data

McCullough, Susan.
    Your new dog : an expert answers your every question / Susan McCullough—
1st ed.
        p.   cm.
    ISBN 1-931868-18-2 (alk. paper)
    1. Dogs.   2. Dogs—Miscellanea.   I. Title.
    SF427.M4725   2003
    363.7'0887—dc21

                                                        2002031492

Printed in the United States of America on acid-free paper that meets the American National Standards Institute Z39-48 Standard.

First Edition

10 9 8 7 6 5 4 3 2 1

For Molly, Cory, and the next New Dog

Contents

Acknowledgments

Most books that are credited to a single author are really team efforts —and this book is a case in point. I want to thank all the people and dogs who helped make this book possible, especially:

- The terrific people at Capital Books, especially editors Noemi Taylor and Judy Karpinski and publisher Kathleen Hughes;
- Illustrator Talia Greenberg;
- My agent, Lynn Whittaker;
- All the experts, people, and pooches who inspired my exploration of every topic covered in the Q's and A's;
- And, most especially, my wonderful family: my husband, Stan Chappell; our daughter, Julie Chappell; and our late, great dogs: Molly and Cory.

Your New Dog

Introduction

When I was in my late twenties and living alone, I developed a serious case of maternal longing. Everywhere I looked, I seemed to encounter adorable infants: cute babies, wiggly babies, giggly babies, sweet-smelling babies. I loved cuddling them. I loved talking to them. And I wanted one—badly.

This longing gripped me back in the late 1970s, when social disapproval of unwed mothers was pretty high. I wasn't ready to deal with such disapproval, even to ease my baby hunger. And even if I'd been emotionally ready to thumb my nose at social conventions, my finances dictated that I follow a different course. Simply put, I didn't have the money to raise a child alone.

So I headed to the local animal shelter and got myself a dog.

The canine in question was an adorable ragamuffin of a mixed poodle. But even at the tender age of eight months, she had already had a murky past. Her previous owner had been an elderly person who'd told the staff at the shelter that she didn't have time to care for the dog. But, judging from the way the dog cringed when confronted with the umbrella I'd brought with me, I suspected the animal had been abused.

I had doubts about taking in a dog with such emotional baggage—but she appeared to have no doubts about me. When released from her kennel, she ran straight over to where I was sitting, hopped up onto my lap, and stared into my face. A minute or two later, she jumped off my lap, bounded up the stairs, and looked back at me as if to say, "Okay, I've chosen you. Can we go now?"

There was no way I could say no to this dog's apparent determination that I be her human companion. So the little ragamuffin, whom I named Molly, came home with me a day later, after the shelter had concluded that I would be a suitable guardian for her.

I was determined to be not just a suitable guardian—I was going to be the best guardian on the planet. And in return for my sterling guardianship, I expected Molly to offer me unconditional love whenever I wanted it. I also expected her to accept my daily ten-hour absences with equanimity and to always be totally mellow when I arrived home. I was sure that my childhood experiences with dogs—most of which I recalled as being problem-free—would be duplicated with Molly.

Not all of my expectations were out of line. Molly did appear to love me, no matter how many mistakes I made in caring for her. And boy, I made plenty. For one thing, I didn't know how to housetrain her. In fact, I didn't know how to train her to do much of anything. I certainly didn't know how to deal with her tendency to tear up my apartment while I was at work and to pee all over the floor when I arrived home.

Consequently, for a year or so, Molly and I had a fragile relationship. I loved her, but I hated coming home at night to an apartment that looked like a rock star's hotel room. Equally odious was the need to clean up Molly's "puddles" almost every day. I lost count of the number of times I considered taking her back to the shelter. The only thing that stopped me was the realization that Molly might not find another home—that my giving her up could be tantamount to a death sentence for her.

So Molly and I somehow muddled through. And eventually—I'm not sure how or why—she settled down. The two of us embarked on a fifteen-year adventure together: an adventure in which we moved five times, I got married, and I became the mother of a human child, just as I'd wanted when Molly and I first met each other. Through these and many other changes, Molly was there, happy to just go along wherever my life led us. I wouldn't have traded those fifteen years for anything. But I sure could have done without that first year.

So, in fact, can you.

As my experience with Molly shows, bringing a new puppy or dog into your life can be either one of the most joyous or one of the most frustrating experiences you'll ever have. Although these perceptions are poles apart, often all that separates them are a few expectations—or the lack thereof.

Maybe, like I was, you're looking for someone to nurture, perhaps even a child substitute. Or maybe you're hoping to satisfy a childhood longing for a very special companion: a dog who can be the Rin Tin Tin to your Rusty . . . or the Lassie to your Timmy . . . or the Sandy to your Little Orphan Annie.

Nothing is wrong with any of those expectations. They tap into our deepest memories and reflect desires that are hardwired into our psyches. However, those memories, desires, hopes, and dreams need to be coupled with practical knowledge and understanding. We need to realize that a new dog, as much as he or she will love us and need us, will nevertheless act like a dog . . . not like a human baby, or like a mindless fount of never-ending adoration, or like a cinematic super-canine. We also need to do the homework that enables us to do right by the very real, very individual dogs who come into our lives.

I've written this book to help you develop the knowledge that will provide a reality check for your hopes and dreams about the dog you bring into your life. When you acquire such knowledge, your canine companion can become one of the great loves of your life. Without that knowledge, your relationship could be doomed from the start. And, in fact this relationship starts before you even find your new canine companion. It starts when you ask yourself whether you're truly ready to welcome a dependent dog or puppy into your world.

Asking questions and getting answers is a good way to obtain the knowledge you need in order to choose and raise the dog of your dreams. That's why most of this book is presented in a question-and-answer format. Each chapter starts with a brief, general introduction about the chapter's subject and ends by answering specific questions. The book looks at every aspect of selecting and living with a dog: from deciding whether to get a dog in the first place to figuring out when it's time to say a last good-bye. In between, there's plenty of information about where to look for a dog (and where not to look), equipping your home and yourself for a dog's arrival, dealing with all kinds of health and behavior problems, socializing and educating your dog, and dealing with the inevitable changes that come into both of your lives.

Some of you may be wondering how, since I was such a washout in the first year I lived with Molly, I could possibly write a book on this subject. Two words: twenty years. In that time, I educated myself enough to become a journalist who specializes in topics relating to dogs and other animal companions. Today I write about canines and their care for magazines and newspapers, and I'm also the author of a book about how to housetrain a dog.

Alas, Molly—the dog who started it all—is no longer here. Until recently, I shared my life with a Shetland sheepdog named Cory. Sadly, he died just before this book was published. But he and other dogs I've helped by counseling their owners give me lots of article ideas. And the owners' questions appear throughout this book.

In answering those questions, I've established and followed a few writing rules. One is that there are certain words I will never use. At the top of that list of forbidden words is the word *housebreaking*. When teaching a dog proper potty protocol, you're not breaking anything; you're building a relationship. For that reason, I use the word *house-training* rather than *housebreaking* to describe the art of teaching a dog basic bathroom behavior.

Another convention I subscribe to—contrary to all the editorial style manuals that dictate otherwise—is using personal pronouns to describe our canine companions. In this book, you will never see me describe a dog in terms of what *it* is doing. Even neutered dogs are beings with genders, and they deserve the dignity of being referred to as such. Consequently, I'll refer to a dog as "he," "she," "him," or "her" and indicate possession by using "his," and "hers" on an alternating basis. In using gender-specific pronouns, I don't favor one gender over the other, I simply want to recognize that every dog has a gender.

Finally, while this book is designed to provide you with all the information you need to start off right with your new dog, it's not meant to replace advice from other experts such as veterinarians and animal behaviorists. If the suggestions you read here don't work for you and your new four-legged friend, or if you have a question that this book doesn't address, don't hesitate to contact these or other professionals.

I hope you'll find this book to be a fun but informative primer that helps get life with your new dog off to a great start—the start of a joyous experience together.

CHAPTER 1

Making Sure You're Ready for a New Dog

HAVING A DOG is wonderful—if you really want one and have determined that you're ready to commit the time, money, and patience needed to build a lifelong bond with your canine companion. But all too often, that doesn't happen.

Any reputable dog breeder, animal shelter staffer, or breed rescue volunteer undoubtedly can serve up plenty of horror stories involving people who get dogs for all the wrong reasons. I once interviewed a breeder of Labrador retrievers who'd been appalled to get a woman's request for a chocolate Lab puppy to match the Godiva chocolates she was giving her boyfriend for Valentine's Day. And who hasn't heard about the well-meaning parents who give in to juvenile pleadings and get a dog for the kids—only to find that everyone is too busy to take proper care of the dog? A special variation on the latter scenario is the Christmas puppy who, all too often, ends up at the local animal shelter two or three months later.

These sad examples bring up an important principle: Before you add a dog to your life, you need to think about yourself. Such contemplation isn't an exercise in narcissism. Rather, it's an effort to consider what your life is really like and how that life can be adapted to the needs of a puppy or dog.

What are those needs? They're pretty straightforward: food, shelter, care, training, and companionship.

All dogs need food, shelter, care, training, and companionship.

The needs for food and shelter are obvious; all living beings need food and shelter to ensure their physical survival. And of the dog's five requirements, these two probably are the simplest to fulfill: You buy the dog some food, you keep the dog in your house (please, not in a doghouse). However, not all dog foods are created equal, and neither are all rooms in your abode—at least, not from the dog's point of view. Chapters five and nine elaborate on how to shelter and feed (respectively) your canine companion.

The need for health care is obvious, too. A dog who doesn't feel well can't take herself to the veterinarian; she needs a human guardian who's alert to changes in her body and behavior and gets her to the vet when those changes warrant. Chapter seven outlines some of the symptoms—physical and otherwise—that should prompt you to at least call your local animal doctor.

Training and companionship may not seem as important to a dog's physical survival as food and shelter are. A puppy or dog can certainly get along without knowing how to come when he's called or when he's supposed to do his bathroom business. Similarly, spending day after day being ignored by the people in his life won't literally kill a canine. But a dog without training or companionship is a dog that has a lower quality of life than a dog that is trained and has companions.

Without training, a dog could eventually even lose his life altogether. Consider the untrained pooch who doesn't know when he's supposed to potty and consequently does his business on his family's living room carpet. Such actions won't exactly endear the dog to his people, who understandably won't be thrilled with having to clean up dog waste on a regular basis. And if the potty problems continue, the people may give up on the dog altogether; studies have shown that house-soiling problems figure prominently in people's decisions to surrender their dogs to animal shelters. Once a dog is in a shelter, there's no guarantee that he'll find a new home—and if he doesn't find one, chances are high that he'll be euthanized.

The dog who's ignored by his people also leads a diminished life. That's because dogs are very social beings and want more than anything else to be included in the lives of those with whom they reside. Without such contact, they're likely to rebel—and that rebellion can take the form of behavioral problems such as barking, destructiveness, and hyperactivity. Of course, no one likes living with a noisy, destructive, or overactive canine, so such behavior is not likely to bring the dog the kind of attention he's looking for. Instead, he's likely to be ignored more—when he's not being yelled at. Eventually, if his people become sufficiently frustrated, this dog also may end up in an animal shelter.

Does this mean that there is a certain dog-specific lifestyle that you must have in order to be a fit parent for a puppy or a dog? Fortunately, the answer to that question is no. A dog is remarkably adaptable. He can live happily in a crowded city, an out-in-the-middle-of-nowhere farm, and just about every corner of suburbia. He can be equally content in a one-bedroom apartment or a multi-bedroom mansion. He can live in a pack of two (just your dog and you) or in a pack of twenty-two (for example, a household made up of adults, children, and other pets).

When it comes to determining whether you're ready to bring a dog into your life, what matters isn't so much your specific lifestyle, but whether you're willing to adapt that lifestyle to meet that dog's needs. The answers to the questions asked in this chapter will demonstrate how to do just that.

THE HOME-ALONE APARTMENT DOG

I work all day and live in a city apartment. Does this mean I can't have a dog?

Not at all! Plenty of urban professionals live happily with their canine companions in pocket-sized apartments. I was one; both Molly and I were happy in my one-bedroom condominium once we got past our first-year adjustment woes.

That said, living with a home-alone apartment dog does pose special challenges. These challenges range from adjusting your social life to meet the needs of your dog to finding a way to exercise your dog when there's no fenced yard for him to run around in.

For example, if you like to put in a full day's work and then stop at the local watering hole with your colleagues, you may need to rethink that practice. The same is true with routinely burning the midnight oil in your downtown office. Either way, your dog is still sitting home alone, waiting for a potty break, waiting to be fed, and—most important—waiting to spend some quality time with you. Your failure to appear when your dog expects you to walk through the door can lead to unwanted consequences, such as puddles on the floor and chewed-up furniture.

There are ways around such circumstances, though. If you know you're going to be working late, maybe you can go home for lunch and take your four-legged friend out for a midday pit stop. You can also take your work home with you. Having Fido cuddle up next to you can make the after-hours office toil a lot more bearable.

The same is true with exercising. Just because your urban dog can't wander over hill and dale with you the way Lassie did with Timmy doesn't mean that he should be condemned to a lifetime of being a couch potato. A twice-daily brisk walk of twenty minutes each time and/or some regular sessions in a dog park can go a long way toward siphoning off some of your dog's excess energy.

These are just examples. The bottom line is that if—and it's a big if—you can adjust your routine to accommodate your dog's needs, there's no reason why you can't have a four-legged apartment roommate, even if you're away from each other during the day.

A DOG FOR THE KIDS

Our kids have been bugging us to get them a dog. My husband says that it's okay with him, as long as they do all the dog care work. He thinks that will teach them how to be more responsible. I'm not so sure.

Your uncertainty is appropriate. Parents who buy a dog for a child and expect the child to take charge of the animal's care are setting the family up for failure.

The real issue here is not whether the kids want the dog, but whether you and your spouse do. That's because as the parents, you are the ones who inevitably will be handling most of the dog's care: the walking, the feeding, the cleaning-up-after, the training, and the schlepping of Fido to the vet. Children of any age simply can't be counted on to perform those tasks (although they can certainly help with some).

The age(s) of your child(ren) is also a factor. Even if you desperately want a dog, it's tough to deal with a canine baby when you're also dealing with one or more human babies. Toddlers are problematic, too, because they don't understand that a dog or puppy isn't just another stuffed animal. Consequently, such small children are apt to squeeze or otherwise inadvertently mistreat a dog—especially a small dog —unless their interactions with the dog are under constant parental supervision.

That's why most experts advocate holding off on getting a dog if your children are younger than five or six. At that point, depending on their ages and levels of responsibility, they can begin to perform simple dog-care tasks, such as feeding and watering—with Mom's or Dad's supervision. Still, children younger than teenagers generally need their parents to show them how to perform those simple tasks and to make sure that those tasks actually get done. My own daughter, Julie, has been brushing our dog's teeth since she was about seven. She's now thirteen and she does a great job—but I still have to remind her to do it.

And if you think that once your kids hit their teens and supposedly are more responsible that they'll be able to take over dog care, well, think again. Even if your teen is exceptionally conscientious, he'll be juggling lots of other demands: schoolwork, activities, part-time job, and social priorities. Consequently, you're still likely to be doing most of the dog duty. The bottom line: Never get a dog for the kids. Instead, get the dog for yourself—and then, only if you truly want one.

THE SENIOR CONNECTION

I'm a senior citizen and can't do a lot of walking. But I enjoy dogs and would love to live with one. What's the best type of dog for me?

Probably a dog who doesn't require a lot of walking. Particularly good for you would be a toy-sized dog, such as a miniature poodle, Yorkshire terrier, Lhasa apso, or shih tzu. Those and other similarly diminutive dogs can be housetrained indoors using newspapers, potty pads, or a litter box. Presto! The need for the two-or-three-times-a-day sojourn outdoors is eliminated.

Eliminating the need for daily walks doesn't mean that a little dog can do completely without exercise. What is true, however, is that exercising a pint-sized pooch is considerably easier than exercising a larger one, even for a person who can't get around easily.

An adult dog probably would be a better bet for you than a puppy would be. In general, older dogs have learned all of their bathroom basics and also may be calmer than their juvenile counterparts. In addition, adults can be adopted from shelters, rescue groups, and even breeders for a much lower cost than would be the case if you were to adopt a purebred puppy.

Your interest in living with a dog is an incredibly healthy one, incidentally. Researchers have found that older people who own a dog or other animal companion are more physically active and maintain better emotional health than those who don't live with pets. Many shelters and humane organizations are trying to capitalize on this research by linking senior citizens with appropriate adoptable dogs and offering discounts on adoption fees and other services. You might consider checking with your local shelter to see if such a program is available in your area.

THE FENCELESS FIDO

We live in the suburbs, but we don't have a fence around our backyard—and frankly, after looking at fencing prices, I don't want to get one! Does this mean we can't have a dog?

Of course you can! Plenty of people without fences help their dogs live long and healthy lives. Chances are, though, such people are a lot more careful when they take their dogs outside than are those who have fenced the perimeters of their yards.

If your property isn't fenced, you can't just let your dog out the back door into your yard. You'll need to snap a leash on his collar and walk him whenever he has to potty. And if you want him to get a good run or other strenuous exercise, you'll need to take him to a safe, enclosed area.

That said, a lack of fencing can actually be *good* for your dog. Why? Because the lack of a fence forces you—if you're a responsible dog parent—to be with your dog when he does his bathroom business or canine calisthenics. Dogs are incredibly social creatures; the more they are with their people, the happier they will be.

BYPASSING BATHROOM ISSUES

I'd love to have a puppy, but don't want to go through all the work of housetraining him. What can I do?

Alas, no puppy under the age of six months can housetrain himself. That means you have to do it. But if the idea of teaching potty protocol sounds like more than you want to handle, you've got an alternative: adopting an older puppy or a full-grown dog.

Once a puppy reaches the magic six-month mark, he usually has sufficient control of his bladder to refrain from doing his bathroom business until you tell him it's okay to do so. And in fact, many adoptable dogs over a year old are already housetrained. That means they've mastered their basic bathroom manners and are looking to show you what they can do.

WHEN FIDO OR BABY MAKES FOUR

We're having a baby in a couple of months. Should we get a dog now?

Probably not. A new baby means sleepless nights, days that run into each other, and lots for new parents to learn. Adding the stress of caring for a new dog to the challenge of caring for a new child puts more pressure on new parents than most would care to handle.

But if you already have a dog and are welcoming a new baby into your family, the story is quite different. It's more than possible for everyone in the family—including Fido—to enjoy the new arrival. Chapter sixteen offers tips for helping a dog adjust to sharing his adult people with a new human.

DEALING WITH NO-PETS CLAUSES

I would love to have a dog, but my landlord doesn't allow me to have pets. What can I do?

Before we talk about what you can do, let's talk about what you *shouldn't* do: sneak the dog in and hope the landlord doesn't find out about him. By doing so, you're not only contributing to many landlords' antipathy toward permitting dogs and other pets in their buildings; you also may set yourself up for eviction or even legal action. If you live in a large rental complex that prohibits pets and you're dying to have a dog, you're probably better off moving to a building that is more welcoming to nonhuman beings. And that's not as difficult as it sounds. A determined renter stands a very good chance of finding an apartment building where dogs are permitted to live with their people.

Generally, a successful quest to find a pet-friendly rental home is a matter of networking and self-promotion. Networking can start online at the website for The Humane Society of the United States (www .hsus.org/programs/companion/renting/residents_steps.html). The site not only offers tips for finding pet-friendly apartments, but also links to sites that list specific buildings in various cities. Check, too, with pet-owning friends, rental agents, and real estate agents that you know.

Once you find some likely buildings, be prepared to sell the landlord on your dog's sterling qualities. References from a veterinarian, a dog trainer, or your current landlord can all help convince a prospective landlord that your canine companion will be a model tenant.

And be willing to fork over some extra money. Many complexes that allow dogs and other pets on the premises ask that the renter pay a pet deposit of several hundred dollars plus an additional $15 to $25 per month on the rental fee. The deposit—which usually isn't refundable—covers any damage that a dog might inflict on a rental property. In most cases, it's a reasonable request; the landlord simply wants to protect his property against canine damage or have the means to repair any damage that a dog might incur.

HOW SOON IS TOO SOON?

We had to have our beloved Lab put to sleep a couple of weeks ago, and the house feels so empty without a dog. Is it too soon to get a new one?

There's no single answer to this question—for every grieving individual or family, there's a different response. Often, the bereaved person or family knows better than anyone when it's time to welcome a new dog into the household.

That said, experts offer a few tips if you do decide to bring a new dog into your home. First and foremost, make sure you're working through your grieving process: denial, anger, bargaining, depression, and acceptance. Talking with understanding friends, participating in a pet-loss support group, or just writing your thoughts in a journal can help you come to terms with the loss of your four-legged friend.

Once you're feeling well on the road to recovery—and that could take weeks or months, depending on the individual—give some thought to adopting a dog who's at least somewhat different from the one you lost. For example, if your dearly departed Labrador retriever was a yellow male, consider adopting a black female Lab the next time around. And there's nothing that says you have to stick with Labs. Maybe now's the time to try a new breed. Either way, though, the idea is to make sure that the new dog will have a chance to be appreciated for his own unique qualities and won't be expected to simply replace the dog that passed away.

ARE YOU SURE YOU'RE READY?

The decision to add a dog to your family shouldn't be undertaken lightly. Here are some questions to ask yourself *before* you start melting in front of a pair of winsome canine eyes:

Why do you want a dog? If you simply think it's the thing to do, or you want to end the kids' pestering, you need to reconsider. The only reason to bring a dog into your life is because you really *want* to experience the joy of canine company—and you're willing to take on the work that's entailed in sharing your life with a tail-wagger.

Do you have time for a dog? Caring for a canine is a 24/7 responsibility, every day of the year. Your dog needs to eat, drink, pee, and poop, whether or not you feel like feeding him or walking him. He needs your care and attention no matter how tired you feel, how much you want to stay out and party, how late you have to work, or where you have to ferry the kids in the minivan for the next few hours.

Can you afford a dog? Adopting a dog isn't cheap. If you go to a reputable breeder, you can expect to pay between $500 and $1,000 for a healthy puppy; if you adopt from a shelter, fees can range from $50 to $100. Training, veterinary care, spaying/neutering, grooming, toys, food, licensing, and equipment all cost extra—in many cases, $1,000 per year.

Can you deal with the downside? Dogs make wonderful companions, no question about it. However, they also have toilet accidents and digestive upsets, both of which wreak havoc on carpets. They can be incredibly destructive; in fact, a determined dog can literally eat through a wall. They can be noisy; just ask anyone who's listened to a dog's incessant barking, yelping, or yodeling in the middle of the night. And just like people, they can need expensive emergency medical treatment—as happened the time my Sheltie, Cory, accidentally ingested a sock, which we had to have surgically removed, to the tune of about $1,000.

Are you willing to make a lifetime commitment to this dog? A dog's normal life span ranges between ten and fifteen years — and many live even longer. Try to picture what your life might be like five or ten years from now. If that picture can't be accommodated to fit a dog, then perhaps you shouldn't acquire a canine companion at this time. On the other hand, if—despite all the warnings you've read so far—you can't imagine your life without the pleasure of canine company, consider yourself ready.

CHAPTER 2

Knowing Where to Find Your New Dog

NOW THAT YOU know you want a new dog—and have determined that you're ready for one—where can you find him?

There are plenty of places to look, but some are definitely better than others. When it comes to the better places, there are three main options: reputable breeder, rescue group, and animal shelter. Of these three best bets, none is superior to the other; instead, each meets a different set of demands from would-be dog owners.

Take, for example, the reputable breeder. She's the person to turn to if you know you want a young puppy and you have a specific breed in mind. By contrast, the breed rescue group is your best bet if you've decided on a breed, but don't mind getting an older puppy or adult dog. Finally, the animal shelter is where to turn if you simply want a dog, but are flexible as to age and breed.

All three sources offer definite pluses to the person in search of a canine companion. The advantages of buying your dream dog from a breeder are considerable: for one thing, you'll know exactly what type of puppy or dog you'll be getting. That's because a breeder can show you the genealogy—in breeder-speak, the pedigree—of the puppy you're perusing. You should also be able to meet the puppies' mother. Generally, if you like the mother, you probably will like her offspring.

You also get the benefit of an expert's help in selecting the dog who's just right for you. For example, Cory's breeder steered my family and me to the largest male puppy in the litter. Her reasoning: A large puppy would do better in an active family like ours than a small, quiet puppy would. And she knew we preferred a male. The result was our meeting Cory, who turned out to be just the right dog for us.

Another advantage to working with a good breeder is that the same expertise that helps you find the right dog in the first place can also help you solve whatever problems or challenges you may face with your dog throughout his life. I've stayed in touch with Cory's breeder during the entire seven years he's been with us, because I know she can answer questions that I can't find the answers to myself. And I also know that she wants to keep up with how he's doing.

A great puppy or dog can be found in several places.

There are some downsides to working with a breeder, though. For one thing, the cost of a pedigreed puppy can be daunting to budget-conscious individuals. A breeder generally will charge between $500 and $1,000 for a puppy who's meant to be strictly a pet, and prices above $1,000 are not uncommon. If you're interested in buying a show dog, expect to pay at least $1,000—and to share ownership with the breeder in what may be a complicated contract.

Another disadvantage is that you may have to wait a long time for the purebred puppy or dog that you want. Many breeders actually have waiting lists of eager buyers for puppies that aren't even born yet. And to get on that waiting list, you'll need to provide a refundable deposit of a couple hundred dollars or so.

Finally, many experts contend that purebred dogs are more likely to have genetic diseases than their mixed-breed counterparts. Large-breed dogs, such as Labs and golden retrievers, may encounter muscular-skeletal problems like hip dysplasia; some herding dogs, such as collies and Shelties, have eye problems; and other breeds, like Great Danes and Doberman pinschers, are prone to problems with their hearts. Scientific research is helping breeders to screen dogs for these diseases, so that those dogs who have them or are genetic carriers are not bred. Such research, however, is often a long, slow process—so in the meantime, it's important to know about the special problems the breed of your choice may face, and to make an informed decision.

The best way to find a good breeder is through the referral services of the American Kennel Club, a national breed club (for example, the Collie Club of America, if you're interested in a collie), or a local all-breed kennel club. Many of these referral services are on-line. Start by logging on to the American Kennel Club's on-line breeder referral service at www.akc.org/breeds/breederinfo/breeder_search.cfm, and follow the prompts.

If cost is a consideration but your heart's set on a purebred, a breed rescue group can be a wonderful source for you. These groups are generally made up of breeders and other devotees of a particular breed who almost always volunteer their services. They provide foster care for unwanted dogs of their particular breed and work to find permanent homes for the dogs.

The biggest plus to working with a rescue group is probably knowing that you're giving a homeless dog a second chance to live in a happy home. There's an undeniable satisfaction to knowing that you've helped change the life of a down-on-his-luck dog—a dog who's likely to repay your kindness with even more love and devotion than you could have anticipated.

Then, too, those who foster rescued dogs generally know their foster "kids" pretty well. They can give you a detailed analysis of a given dog's history, pluses, and minuses. They're likely to know, for example, that Doggie X would do better in a home without children, while Doggie Y is a canine Houdini who needs a home with an escape-proof fence.

And, as I mentioned earlier, purebred rescue dogs cost much less than those who come from breeders—generally no more than $200. Those charges cover the costs of spaying or neutering the dog and any medical care the animal needs. The rescue group doesn't profit from these minimal fees (which many groups prefer to call donations).

That's not to say that getting a dog from a rescue group is problem free. Many of these dogs come with some emotional baggage that expresses itself in the form of behavioral problems. It's important to find out from the dog's foster family whether the animal you're considering has any fears, phobias, or training challenges that may have landed him at the rescue group in the first place. Then, once you find out what your dog's issues are, you need to figure out how you're going to address them—and to commit yourself to doing so. That commitment can be as simple as spending more time with the dog than you might otherwise have anticipated, or as complicated as working one-on-one with a trainer or animal behaviorist to solve your dog's special problems.

Finding a breed rescue group in your immediate area starts with logging on to the AKC website at www.akc.org/breeds/rescue.cfm. From there, scroll down the list of breed clubs until you come to the breed of your choice. There, you'll find a national rescue contact who can direct you to a local breed rescue group.

In addition, some rescue groups can help you find a dog who lives outside your local area and arrange to have the animal transported to you. If you're interested in this possibility, ask the rescue coordinator about whether the group operates a "Canine Underground Railroad" or whether there's some other way you can find out more about rescue dogs who live beyond your local area.

The same satisfaction that comes from adopting a dog from a breed rescue group can also be yours if you adopt a dog from an animal shelter. These days, most local shelters have come a long way from being the dire dog pounds of yore. They not only offer dogs, cats, and other animals second chances to find new homes, many also offer services such as low-cost spaying and neutering, low-cost immunizations, and even dog training for canine adoptees and their people.

No source offers a greater variety of dogs to choose from than a shelter does. The Humane Society of the United States estimates that one-third of the dogs in shelters are purebreds—which means that the other dogs are likely to be, both individually and collectively, a wide-ranging mix of breeds. And all shelter dogs cost much less than the puppy or dog you buy from a reputable breeder.

Some people hesitate to adopt a dog from a shelter because other people have already rejected the dog. Such fears are unfortunate, because shelters offer some terrific dogs for the choosing. More often than not, dogs are relinquished because their human caretakers are irresponsible, not because the dog is inherently bad or inferior.

TABLE 2.1 DOG SOURCES AT A GLANCE

Source	Pros	Cons
Reputable Breeder	Good source of knowledge Dogs' histories are known Dogs likely to be healthy Best selections of purebred pups Health guarantees	Expensive Sometimes hard to find and approach Pups not always available
Animal Shelter	Saves lives Less expensive than breeders or rescue groups Best selection of adult dogs Best selection of mixed breeds	Few puppies Few purebreds Dogs' histories not always known Dogs not always totally healthy Dogs may have emotional issues
Rescue Group	Saves lives Dogs' histories often known Both purebred and mixed dogs Less expensive than breeders Good selection of adult dogs Dogs given good care	Few puppies Dogs not always totally healthy Dogs may have emotional issues
Pet Store	Very convenient No waiting period before purchase Good selection of puppies	Dogs often overpriced Dogs often come from puppy mills Dogs may not be healthy Few guarantees
Classified Ads	Convenient Often no waiting period before purchase	Advertiser reputation may be unknown Dogs may not be healthy Guarantees questionable

That said, some shelter dogs may have behavioral problems—and those behavioral problems sometimes don't show up right away. You may not know, for example, that your dog is terrified of thunderstorms until you get home.

And unlike people who work with rescue groups, shelter personnel may not know a whole lot about the dogs in their care. Those who've been picked up as strays, in fact, come with no histories at all. Those who are surrendered by their previous owners may not bring much information, either. That's because an owner often gives a reason for relinquishment that has little to do with the real factors behind the decision to bring the dog to the shelter. And because shelter workers often have more dogs to care for than rescue volunteers do, they may not have time to truly get to know their canine charges.

Still, most communities have local animal shelters that are happy —make that thrilled—to find homes for the dogs in their care. If you're interested in adopting a dog from a shelter, pay it a visit. But be prepared to be very tough-minded; don't let yourself be swayed by the first pair of big brown puppy eyes you see. Know what you want and don't say "yes" to any dog unless doing so feels absolutely right.

Following is some more information to help you determine where to find the dog of your dreams.

GOOD VERSUS BAD BREEDERS

How can I tell the difference between a reputable breeder and one that's not so reputable?

One of America's best-known dog trainers (and dog authors), Brian Kilcommons, answers this question very simply by saying, "The mark of a good breeder is truth."

In other words, a good breeder is truthful with would-be buyers. She'll tell you what genetic problems or diseases her breed is prone to. She'll be up front about explaining why one puppy from a litter would be a better match for you than another puppy from the same litter would be. She'll show you the puppies' pedigrees, so that you can see exactly how they were bred. And she'll be proud to show you exactly how and where she raises her puppies and to have you meet their mother (in breeder-speak, the puppies' dam).

When she shows you around her home, you'll see that it's clean.

You'll notice that the puppies are being raised inside the home, so that they can become comfortable with people. And when you ask her how many litters she raises each year, she'll say something like, "Only two or three—I'm not doing this to make money."

She also invests the time and money needed to make sure that the dogs she breeds are healthy. To the maximum extent possible, she tests those dogs to make sure that they are free from genetic diseases or problems. The "Testing, Testing . . ." box describes some of the more common tests performed on puppies or dogs, and why they're important.

When you ask the breeder whether she shows her dogs, she'll point proudly to the championships her dogs have won at dog shows and maybe to the titles they've won for herding, obedience competitions, agility, flyball, or other dog sport. Those accolades will tell you that

TESTING, TESTING . . .

The key to breeding healthy purebred puppies is to ensure that their parents are free of genetic disease. That's why good breeders screen their animals for conditions that can afflict dogs, literally, from head to toe.

One such test is administered by the Orthopedic Foundation for Animals (OFA). This screening rates a dog's hips and elbows to see if the joints have developed properly. If the joints have developed incorrectly, conditions called hip dysplasia or elbow dysplasia can result. Either type of dysplasia can be extremely painful to a dog and could result in irreversible, crippling arthritis. Large breeds are especially prone to this condition, but sometimes smaller dogs—for example, a twenty-pound Shetland sheepdog—get it, too.

A good breeder whose animals are at risk for hip or elbow dysplasia will have those dogs' hips rated by the time they're two years old. And she'll be happy to provide the OFA ratings certificates to you.

Similar tests for eye diseases are administered by the Canine Eye Registry Foundation (CERF).

she's serious about breeding the best possible dogs and that she values the judgment of her fellow breeders.

Finally, the reputable breeder will want to stay in touch with you after she sells you a puppy. She'll tell you to feel free to call her for help at any point during your puppy's life—even if that point occurs years after her puppy joins your family.

By contrast, the not-so-reputable breeder will disappear—or at least will refuse to take your calls—once he's gotten your money. He'll try to tell you that the breed he raises has no genetic problems (run, don't walk, if you hear such a claim). He'll say that breeding is a good way to make money—and you'll be able to tell that he doesn't spend much of that money on keeping his facility clean. In fact, you probably won't see many puppies (if any) being raised inside his house. Instead, you'll see them in outdoor kennels, isolated from the sights and sounds of a human home. A question about whether he shows his dogs will be met by a blank stare.

The bottom line here is that a good breeder cares about making great dogs, while a casual or backyard breeder probably cares mainly about making money. When it comes to finding a purebred puppy that will become the dog of your dreams, look for a breeder who clearly focuses on the dog, not the dollar.

THE DOG SHOW CONNECTION

I've always heard that if you're looking for a purebred dog, it's a good idea to go to dog shows and talk to breeders. But when I tried to do that at a dog show last week, none of the breeders seemed to want to talk to me: They gave me one-word answers and generally just blew me off. What's going on?

In a word (well, four, but who's counting?): Those breeders were busy. They're so preoccupied with getting their dogs ready to step into the ring that they simply can't focus on answering the questions of a person they've just met—even if that person is interested in buying one of their dogs. They just don't have time to talk at the particular moment.

Does this mean that you should avoid dog shows if you're looking for a purebred puppy? Absolutely not: A dog show is a great place to find breeders to talk to *later*. Consider asking for the breeder's business card and following up with a phone call a day or two later.

Another option is to cough up a few dollars for the show catalog, which will list the names and addresses of each competing dog's breeder. Use that information to write to the breeders of dogs who catch your eye, and develop a relationship from there.

PUPPY LOVE IN THE CLASSIFIEDS

Can't I find a puppy or dog in the classified ads section of my newspaper?

A few years ago, I would have answered that question, "Absolutely not." I would have said that good breeders don't need to advertise their upcoming litters; generally, such breeders have waiting lists for their dogs. And that's still true.

However, some animal shelters and breed rescue groups—particularly those in large metropolitan areas—have begun to promote their available dogs via classified newspaper ads. Such groups will usually leave more than a phone number with their ad, though. They'll identify themselves as being, say, the "Tri-County Animal Shelter" or "Montgomery County Golden Retriever Rescue." By contrast, an ad from a not-so-reputable breeder will probably provide only a telephone number.

So, today, it's fair to say that you can find true puppy love in the classifieds—if you're careful and ignore advertisements from breeders. By sticking with ads from shelters and rescue groups, you stand a better chance of finding your dream dog.

WHY SPAY AND NEUTER?

No matter where I turn—breeder, shelter, or rescue group—they all demand that I spay or neuter any dog I adopt. Why?

All three sources tend to be pretty insistent about spaying and neutering. And all three have good reasons—although those reasons differ somewhat from place to place.

A good breeder's reason for being a breeder is simple: to produce the best possible puppies that she can. That raison d'être would be undermined considerably if any puppies other than the best were to have offspring of their own.

Take, for example, my own dog, Cory the Super Sheltie. To me, naturally, he is a vision of perfection, but to show people, his flaws are considerable. Shelties who show are supposed to be no bigger than sixteen inches high at the shoulder; Cory tops eighteen inches. Moreover, his ears stick straight up (in show parlance, they're prick ears); show Shelties' ears should bend over at the tips. Both Cory's height and ear carriage are considered to be faults that disqualify him from the show ring, and Cory's breeder didn't want those imperfections perpetuated in any offspring. Hence, she required us to have him neutered.

All three sources—breeders, shelters, and rescue groups—have an especially compelling reason to require spaying and neutering: to reduce canine overpopulation. As many as two-thirds of the dogs who enter animal shelters never leave. That's because if they're not adopted within a few days or weeks of arrival, they're often euthanized to make room for the next batch of dogs that are arriving. The same fate awaits those in the new group who aren't among the quickly chosen. This is a tragic waste of life and potential—not just for the dogs, but for the people with whom those dogs might have shared a deep, lifelong bond if they'd had the chance.

Breed rescue groups don't euthanize adoptable animals; instead, they foster them in individual homes until their "forever" home materializes. But most rescue groups are small and have very limited funding. Consequently, they can help only a few dogs at a time. Requiring adopters to spay or neuter their canine adoptees helps to prevent any rescue dogs' offspring from finding their way back to the rescue group, and thus holds rescue numbers down over the long term.

SCREENING WOULD-BE OWNERS

Some breeders, adopters, and rescue groups make you jump through as many hoops as you have to when you adopt a child! Why are they so fussy?

Because they want their puppies and dogs to live long and happy lives with people who love them. And the only way they know of to be sure of that is to check and double-check the backgrounds of those who want to adopt their precious pooches.

Author and dog show judge Chris Walkowicz of Sherrard, Illinois, who also is a former breeder, puts it this way: "Even when our [human] children grow up and leave our homes, we always want the best for them. For breeders the same is true for our puppies. I live in terror that one of my babies will be neglected, abused, or placed into the wrong hands."

Animal shelters and breed rescue groups are just as determined to place the canines in their care with responsible, loving homes. After all, the canines in their charge already have had at least one home that didn't work out. Many of the dogs they're trying to place may have suffered neglect and physical abuse. The groups who are trying to save these dogs' lives naturally will do everything in their power to ensure that the next homes these dogs go to will be their "forever" homes.

If those considerations aren't enough to make you reconsider the importance of jumping through those hoops, here's some more food for thought: One mark of a good breeder, shelter, or rescue group is that they ask you as many questions as you ask them. In other words, if you're being put through the third degree in your quest to adopt a dog or puppy, you can feel confident that the animal you adopt will be one that's right for you.

WHY NOT GET THAT DOGGIE IN THE WINDOW?

Every time I pass the pet store at the local shopping mall, my heart melts: There are so many cute puppies there! And it's so much easier to buy a purebred puppy there than wait forever on a breeder's waiting list. Why shouldn't I buy a puppy from a pet store?

All that's really needed to answer this question are two words: puppy mills.

Many, if not all, of the dogs that are sold in mall-based pet stores come from puppy mills, which are the worst of all possible breeding operations. Whereas the reputable breeder works with just one or two breeds and raises only a few litters a year, the puppy mill has scores of breeds and raises litters 24/7, every day of the year. The reputable breeder is usually a hobbyist dedicated to improving a specific breed; the puppy mill is a business aimed strictly at making money.

Making money isn't a bad thing in and of itself, of course. But these operations make their money by making innocent animals miserable. Female dogs are forced to mate as often as possible, and litters are raised under horrendous conditions. Often the dogs are kept in very small cages, piled one on top of the other. The dogs have very little room to stand, much less turn around. They often must be accustomed to living in their own bodily wastes, which completely short-circuits the dog's instinctive desire to keep itself clean.

Not surprisingly, puppy mill puppies often aren't in the best of health. Because their breeders pay little attention to basic care, much less genetics and inherited diseases, the puppies that emerge from these operations are quite likely to have health problems from the get-go. They may also have behavioral problems, particularly if—as often is the case—they're not socialized at the times they should be. A seven-week-old puppy who should be frolicking with her littermates and gradually learning about the world around her is more likely, if she comes from a puppy mill, to be stuck in a shipping crate that's being trucked from the mill to a pet store.

I know those stores are convenient. And I know those puppies are hard to resist. Plus, the pet stores take plastic and let you take your precious new pooch home right away. Unfortunately, though, when you give in to that kind of convenience, you may open a Pandora's box of problems that not only are inconvenient but also can be heartbreaking. Those difficulties include health problems, behavioral problems, and—all too often—premature death.

It's better to avoid such heartbreak in the first place. The best way to do that is to resist all those cute, cuddly, sad-eyed canine temptations that the mall pet shop dangles in front of you. Delay your gratification now so that you'll have a healthy dog later—and for longer.

MYTHS ABOUT BREEDERS

If I buy a puppy from a breeder, aren't I contributing to the pet overpopulation problem? Wouldn't I be doing dogs a whole lot more good if I were to adopt one from a shelter or rescue group?

The answer to that question depends on what sort of breeder you're buying from. If you're confining your search to reputable breeders, you've got nothing to feel guilty about. Buying from a reputable breeder—an individual or couple who care about the breed and clearly don't expect to make a lot of money—doesn't really affect the population of homeless dogs for good or ill.

That's because a healthy purebred dog is much less likely to end up in a shelter or to be abandoned than the product of a puppy mill, backyard breeder, or chance encounter between two randy canines. Caring breeders choose their puppies' parents carefully, raise the puppies in their own loving homes, and choose their puppies' future homes with great deliberation. They also generally insist—and they put that insistence into their contracts—that if a puppy or dog does not work out, that the animal be returned to them. The population of dogs that breeders work with generally doesn't mix with the population of dogs that find themselves abandoned or in shelters.

That said, adopting from a shelter does produce the unquestionable satisfaction of having saved a dog's life. Similarly, adopting a dog from a breed rescue group brings the adopter the knowledge that she's improved the life of a pooch that's probably had more than his fair share of hard knocks.

FINDING A DOG ON-LINE

Janine Adams, a St. Louis writer who specializes in all things canine, would be the first to agree that breeders, shelters, and rescue groups are great places to find great dogs. But she's also found a fourth source for learning about dogs and even, occasionally finding one: the vast world of cyberspace, otherwise known as the World Wide Web.

Adams has good reason for her conviction: She found her three-year-old poodle, Pip, through a Web-based rescue service. For her, using the Web to find her canine companion was a no-brainer.

"I do all my research over the Internet, so this just seemed natural," Adams says. "I also knew of plenty of long-distance adoptions, so it didn't seem at all unusual to start looking for my new dog over the Internet."

Adams knew she wanted a young adult female standard poodle, and by scouring several websites on a daily basis, she soon found a likely candidate on Petfinder.com. "They have a fabulous interface," Adams says. "Rescuers or shelters post info on their dogs, and users can easily and quickly search based on breed, or geography, or other characteristic."

Once she settled on Pip, Adams drove to Utah, where Pip was being cared for. Today, the two are living happily ever after with Adams's husband in St. Louis.

What advice would Adams give to others who would surf the Web in search of their dream dogs? "Make sure the dog is coming from a reputable source," she emphasizes. "The group you get the dog from should screen you, just like a local group would." Good sources are those that are affiliated with a national humane organization or a local animal shelter. Sites run by individuals, or that focus on bids or auctions, should be bypassed.

Adams also feels that it's crucial to see the dog in the flesh before finalizing the adoption. "If I got there and she [the dog] turned out to have been misrepresented in some way, I'd have been able to walk away from the deal," she explains.

Any other suggestions? As with any effort to find a dog, Adams recommends that you "Be patient. And trust your gut."

CHAPTER 3

Choosing Your New Dog

YOU'RE AT THE breeder's, or at the animal shelter, or inside the home of a breed rescue volunteer. Greeting you are a half dozen adorable puppies, a dozen or more barking dogs, or maybe just one or two pooches whose sad-looking eyes tell you they've been a little bit down on their luck. And you can't imagine how you can choose just one dog from among the many deserving animals you see.

No matter where you decide to look for your new dog, it's tough to choose one over another. Selecting your future canine companion calls for a lot of objectivity and a little bit of tough-mindedness—neither of which comes easily when you're confronted by one or more sweet doggie faces. But knowing what to look for in a puppy or dog can help, starting from the top down.

If you're picking a puppy from a reputable breeder, here's what to look for:

Clear, bright eyes. Check to see that the puppy can follow a moving object with his eyes; failure to do so may indicate blindness.

Discharge or cloudiness may be a sign of infection or other eye problems.

Dry, odorless ears. Ears that smell like baking bread may have a yeast infection; other odors also indicate infection is present. Clap your hands to see whether the pup responds to the sound; failure to respond may indicate a hearing problem.

Clean skin and full coat. A puppy shouldn't have any scabs or dirt on his skin, and he shouldn't have any bald spots on his coat. Check the mother, too; although she's likely to have a thinner coat than usual due to the hormonal and other changes of motherhood, she shouldn't have any scabs, bald spots, or rashes. Check, too, for fleas (little dark specks that hop around on the coat); if the mother or the puppies have them, it's likely that they haven't gotten the care they should have.

Normal movement. Watch how the puppies walk and run and make sure that they're not having any difficulty. A puppy who limps or appears to lack energy may have health problems that you probably don't want to take on.

Sound temperament. Puppies' personalities vary from breed to breed, and even from dog to dog. Some are reserved, preferring to take their time to get to know people. Others are more outgoing, displaying a hi-how-are-you attitude to everyone they meet. But Mike Richards, a veterinarian who has provided on-line advice to America Online subscribers and others, provides advice that any puppy buyer can apply: "The puppies that are confident enough to come up to a stranger and who seem friendly when they [the puppies] decide to approach are probably the puppies most likely to continue to have good temperaments." In other words, the puppy who chooses you may be your best bet.

If you're looking for your dream dog at a shelter or a rescue group, you can apply guidelines that are similar to those for assessing the

When picking a puppy, pay special attention to the pup who chooses you.

purebred puppy—but be ready to be a little more flexible when it comes to considering the dog's physical health. For example, if you see a pooch with a scab or two on his skin, or ears that smell like baking bread, don't automatically rule him out. Unlike the carefully nurtured purebred puppy, a shelter dog or rescue dog has gotten his share of hard knocks, which can lead to minor health issues such as pyoderma (a skin rash) or a yeast infection (an ear ailment). Such maladies generally clear up quickly after a visit to a veterinarian and the correct use of some prescription meds.

Assessing a shelter dog's or rescue dog's temperament also might require more flexibility than is the case with a reputable breeder's lovingly nurtured puppy. Experiences of abandonment, neglect, and even abuse can cause an otherwise healthy dog to be anxious, hyperactive, or a little shy, but such a dog shouldn't be ruled out automatically.

On the other hand, signs of aggressiveness or extreme shyness should bring a thumbs-down. The pooch who cringes in the corner, lunges at your shoulder, growls menacingly, or literally puts some teeth into his interactions with you should draw an automatic veto, no matter how much you like his other characteristics.

THE LESS-THAN-PERFECT POOCH

We've seen some sweet dogs at our local animal shelter, but there's been something wrong with each: Some are hyperactive, some cower in the corner, and some just don't seem totally healthy. We really like the idea of adopting from a shelter and saving a dog's life, but we want a dog who doesn't have any problems. Are we asking the impossible?

You might be. Leslie Sinclair, DVM, former director of companion animal issues for The Humane Society of the United States, says that "when you adopt from a shelter, you need to think about how the animal got there. The puppies and dogs there generally come from people who could not give these animals the care that they needed. They all need some rehabilitation after they're adopted." Despite such challenges, though, many dogs who come from shelters and rescue groups eventually become splendid canine companions.

You might consider adjusting your expectations a bit. Figure out which challenges you can take on and which challenges feel beyond your experience or inclination. For example, an inexperienced person could probably handle the needs of a shelter dog who has a case of worms. Helping this puppy simply means a couple of trips to the vet for an examination and some deworming medication—not a big deal.

Temperament troubles are a little trickier to evaluate. Many dogs' personalities appear to change when they're subjected to the noise and confinement of even the very best animal shelters. Some react by being fearful; others, by appearing to go berserk. If you're interested in either type of dog, try taking him to a quiet room to get better acquainted; many shelters have rooms for just that purpose. Talk quietly to the dog and see how he reacts. You might be pleasantly surprised.

On the other hand, watch for signs of problems that might be difficult or impossible to fix. For example, a dog who's exuberant can be taught to settle down, but a dog who growls at you or any family member just might be too dangerous to take a chance on.

No matter where you find a dog, there's no foolproof way to avoid problems. As Leslie Sinclair says, it's important to "realize a dog won't be perfect the day you bring him home. You have the responsibility to help him become the dog you want him to be."

CONTRACTS 101

Do I need a contract if I buy a puppy from a breeder? If so, what should be in that contract?

Any purchase of a puppy from a breeder should be formalized with a written contract. Such documents protect the puppy and clarify the rights and responsibilities of both buyer and breeder.

Janice Hicks, an Elgin, Illinois, attorney who specializes in animal law, recommends that buyers check any purchase contracts for the following provisions:

- Clear, specific warranties. "In a contract I would look for express warranties regarding health, vaccinations, history (where the dog comes from), training (if the dog is supposed to be trained for a specific purpose and the extent of that training), pedigree, and quality (pet versus show)," Hicks says.
- Return provisions. "Most 'good' breeders will take one of their dogs back no matter what, even if the dog is several years old," Hicks says. "In my opinion, the best breeders have a provision in their contracts regarding 'right of first refusal,' meaning that if an owner were going to give up a dog, that owner would have to contact the breeder and give the breeder the first right to take or purchase the dog."

• Health contingencies. At the very least, a contract should let a buyer return a dog to the breeder if the animal gets sick shortly after the sale or becomes ill due to a congenital defect. Hicks prefers that a contract allow for the exchange of a sick dog for a healthy one, or a provision that allows the owner to keep the sick dog and be reimbursed for reasonable veterinary costs incurred in trying to cure the animal.

CONTRACTS: TAKE TWO

Will I have to sign a contract if I get a dog from a rescue group or an animal shelter? If so, what's it likely to say?

Contracts between new pet owners and either shelters or rescue groups are likely to spell out what the new owners' obligations are to the pet. These stated obligations vary from group to group, but most require the following from the adopter:

• Spaying or neutering of the dog within a designated time period, usually thirty days. Some groups demand that the adopter place a refundable spay/neuter deposit at the time of adoption.
• Agreement to keep the dog indoors as a pet. That means no chaining, no doghouses, and no use of the dog for other purposes such as breeding or (God forbid) dog fights.
• Return of the dog to the shelter or rescue group if the adopter is no longer able to care for the dog.
• Assuming responsibility for the dog's health and behavior once the adoption is complete.

Appendix two contains two actual adoption contracts: one from an animal shelter, the other from a breed rescue group. Each typifies the agreements that these organizations require from adopters of the dogs in their care.

BRINGING THE KIDS

Should I bring my kids along when it's time to pick out a dog?

Absolutely! Choosing a dog for the family should be a decision the whole family makes. Everyone in the household will have to live with this animal—so it's only fair that everyone who's in a position to have a say in this decision get to share his or her opinion.

Bringing the kids along can also help you see which dogs get along best with your children. The bossy dog that you feel capable of handling might prove to be too assertive for your youngsters to live with safely. The quiet dog who's perfect for someone who lives alone might feel overwhelmed by a passel of children. Either way, it's better for everyone to find these things out before you bring the dog home, rather than after.

And before you all head out to pick your pooch, check to make sure that the breeder, shelter, or rescue group you're visiting will place their dogs in households with children. Some individuals or organizations, particularly rescue groups, limit their adoptions to families with children over the age of six, or even older.

MEETING THE PARENTS

Should I try to meet the parents of the puppy I'm considering? What if I can only meet the puppy's mother?

Meeting one of your puppy's parents can tell you a lot not only about your possible dream dog but also about the breeder from whom you may buy him. Some time spent with your puppy's mother can give you a glimpse of your puppy's future; you can see how he'll look and how he'll act when he reaches adulthood. If you like the mama, chances are you're going to like her offspring just as much tomorrow as you do today.

However, if your breeder tells you that both parents are on the premises, proceed with caution. Find out if they are from two different kennels. If they're not—in other words, if the breeder tells you that both dogs are hers—consider finding another breeder. Chances are, the two dogs are related rather closely to each other. Thus, a breeder who breeds two dogs from her own kennel may be less concerned about genetics and sound breeding than she should be. A good breeder usually looks outside her own kennels to other reputable breeders for potential mates for her dogs. By doing so, she stands a better chance of breeding a litter that enhances the breed's positive characteristics.

GETTING THE THIRD DEGREE

Some people have told me to expect a lot of questions from the breeders or rescue people I visit while I look for a new dog. What exactly are they likely to ask me?

Here's a rundown of questions breeders, shelter personnel, and rescue volunteers often pose to those who are interested in their dogs:

- Why do you want a dog? There are lots of right answers here, such as wanting to give and receive unconditional love, wanting to have someone to nurture, wanting company. Wrong answers include wanting to teach the kids responsibility (they shouldn't be practicing on a helpless dog) and looking for protection (responsible breeders and others will explain that there are other, better ways to protect one's property than trying to turn a dog into a living security system).
- Why are you interested in this breed? Breeders and rescue volunteers who ask you this question are looking for answers that show you've done some homework and know something about the breed you're interested in. (To start doing that homework, check out appendix one in this book.)

- Who will be primarily responsible for the dog's care? The right answer here is "me," "my spouse," "Mom," or "Dad." The wrong answer is "the kids" or "my child." No child of any age should be saddled with primary care for a dog.

- Have you ever owned a dog before? Don't despair if your answer is "no." Either way, your response to this question provides a valuable clue as to what type of dog is best for you.

- How will you exercise this dog? Good answers: walking three or four times a day on a leash, letting him out into our fenced yard. Poor answer: letting him out to run around the neighborhood.

- Do you have children—and if so, how old are they? Don't worry: In most cases, having children won't take you out of contention for a dog (although some breeders of very small dogs such as Chihuahuas may hesitate). But, as with many of the other questions, the answers to this one will help in determining which dog is best for you and your family.

- Does anyone in your household have allergies? It's hard to be happy when one member of a household causes another member to sneeze, sniffle, or break out in hives. Still, many people with animal allergies can live happily with dogs, if they're willing to make certain adjustments. Those adjustments might include restricting one's search to curly coated breeds, such as poodles or Portuguese water dogs; cleaning and vacuuming the house more often; and keeping the dog out of the allergic person's bedroom.

- Does your living situation permit a dog (e.g., does the buyer's lease allow her to have a dog in her apartment?)? There's only one right answer here: yes. And you should be prepared to show proof—documents showing that you own your home or that your landlord allows you to keep a dog.

- How do you feel about taking your dog for training and obedience classes? Again, there's only one right answer: "I think it's important." No matter what his age is, every dog lives more happily with people when he has a little training in basic manners.

- How often will someone be home to care for the dog? The minimal answer here should be in the mornings and evenings—and, if you're getting a puppy, midday as well.
- Do you have a veterinarian, or do you know of one? An affirmative answer to either of these questions shows that there's professional care readily available for the dog you're considering adopting.

THE HOUSE CHECK

The shelter from which I'm adopting my dog wants to send someone to my apartment and see an actual copy of my lease. Why? Don't they believe me when I tell them it's okay for me to have a dog here?

No, they don't. Don't take that skepticism personally, though. Shelters simply have been duped too often. So many dogs are relinquished to shelters because their owners got caught violating no-pets leases that the shelters aren't taking any chances. The shelter personnel want to see for themselves that your apartment is suitable for a dog and that your landlord has given a thumbs-up to canine tenants. If you've been honest in your application, you've got nothing to worry about. In fact, you can use the shelter person's visit to your home as another opportunity to ask questions about dog care in general and your soon-to-be-own dog in particular.

A BREEDER'S VETO

I've picked the dog I want, but the breeder says she won't sell that dog to me. Why?

There are at least a couple of possible reasons. One is that the breeder feels that the pooch you've picked simply isn't the right one for you.

Perhaps, for example, you've chosen a headstrong, assertive dog who the breeder believes would do better with a more experienced owner than you are. Or perhaps you've fallen in love with a shy little darling who needs a home that's quieter than your houseful of kids.

Another reason is that you may have chosen a dog that the breeder feels is destined for greatness in the show ring. If that's the case, the breeder may want to keep the dog for herself in order to show him, or perhaps sell the dog to another breeder. Unless you're willing to schlep a dog to shows every weekend—or pay a professional handler some significant bucks to do that schlepping—you're better off sticking with pet-quality puppies.

In any case, though, you should ask your breeder why she won't sell you a particular dog. If her explanation makes sense, respect her judgment. If you don't like what you hear, you shouldn't hesitate to take your business elsewhere.

A PARTNER'S VETO

My partner and I have been looking for a dog for months. Finally, at the animal shelter this past weekend, I found a dog to fall in love with: a young Border collie/Australian shepherd mix. But my partner not only isn't in love, he's adamant about not wanting the dog. What can I do?

Every dog deserves to be loved by every person in his household—and every person in the household deserves to feel good about the new canine resident. Consequently, if your partner really doesn't care for the dog you've taken such a liking to, I'd go along with his veto—as difficult at that may be. It's worth taking the time to find a pooch that you *both* fall in love with.

You can cut that time a little, though, by talking with your partner about what he wants in a dog and exactly why he objected to the dog you wanted. Maybe the dog was too hyper (herding breeds are often very active). Maybe your partner wants a bigger dog, a smaller dog, or a quieter dog. See where his doggie wish list dovetails with yours. Once you do, subsequent searches should go a lot more smoothly.

If, however, you've both agreed on the type of dog you want but he keeps vetoing your choices, you may face another problem: his possible reluctance to get a dog at all. That's an issue that the two of you need to hash out and come to some agreement on before you make any more trips to the shelter.

GOING WITH YOUR HEART

Everyone tells me I shouldn't pick the runt of the litter, but I love little dogs. Why shouldn't I go with my heart?

Advice can help you make important decisions—but advice isn't everything. It's important to consider who's giving you those suggestions (including those you get from this book!) and to figure out what prompted them.

Not so long ago, when most people got their puppies from a farmer's backyard, the smallest member of the litter was also often the weakest, most unhealthy member of the litter—both physically and emotionally. This little litter member, generally known as the runt, often got pushed around by her larger siblings. She might have had last dibs on her mother's milk because her sibs would serve themselves first. The perpetual pushing around might have prompted her to stay in the background so that she wouldn't be picked on. The result would have been a timid, fearful, unhealthy puppy who—despite her obvious appeal—could pose significant problems to her people. Fearful dogs are sometimes snappish dogs, and dogs who are unhealthy during puppyhood may not see any improvement if they reach adulthood. And if they do live long enough to grow up, their adulthood may not last very long.

Today, though, such scenarios are much less likely, if you purchase your puppy from a reputable breeder. That's because the random breedings that occurred in the past are giving way, slowly but surely, to carefully planned couplings between dogs selected for sound temperament and good health. Consequently, when it comes to picking a puppy, size doesn't matter so much anymore.

In my dog Cory's litter, for example, the smallest puppy was also the feistiest, prompting my daughter and me to dub the dog "Little Miss Hell-Raiser." She didn't seem to have any problem getting her fair share of food, attention, or anything else. We didn't choose her, though; we wanted a dog who was a little quieter and more oriented to people. That dog was Cory—who also, interestingly, was the largest puppy in his litter.

What does this mean for you? Take all that advice under advisement (pun fully intended). In the end, it's okay to follow your heart— as long as you do so with your eyes wide open.

LEARNING THE LINGO

Just as travel to a foreign country improves if the traveler learns a little bit of the native language, communication with a breeder improves if the buyer takes the time to learn some dog-breeding terminology. Here are some examples of breeder-speak, and what they mean:

A show puppy. If a breeder refers to a "show-quality puppy," she's saying that, in her judgment, this puppy possesses the qualities and attributes needed to succeed as a show dog. The breeder may also say that such a dog meets the breed standard: a written description by the national breed club of what constitutes the perfect example of the breed.

A pet-quality puppy. A pet-quality puppy lacks at least one of the attributes needed to do well in the show ring. Such attributes have nothing to do with the dog's health, behavior, or ability to be a loyal and loving pet. For example, a Shetland sheepdog puppy might be considered a pet-quality animal if he's relatively big for his age. That's because the breed standard specifies that a fully grown Sheltie must not be more than sixteen inches high at the shoulder. However, there's no reason that such a dog—commonly referred to as an "oversized" Sheltie—can't be a terrific pet.

"This puppy is a little much." According to Nancy Matlock, an official of the American Kennel Club, a breeder who uses this phrase is probably saying that such a puppy has a strong personality, is relatively independent, and needs more careful handling and experienced care than other puppies might.

"This puppy is very sweet but not as outgoing." Here, says Matlock, the breeder might be saying that such a puppy is too shy to do well in a particular setting, such as an active home with noisy children.

"This puppy is a little bossy." The breeder could be warning that a particular puppy is relatively dominant and needs an experienced owner, Matlock says.

"This puppy is busy." This is breeder-speak for saying a particular dog is very active. "He may be cute to watch but may not be desirable for an inexperienced owner," Matlock explains.

CHAPTER 4

Shopping for Your New Dog

ONGRATULATIONS! YOU'VE FOUND the dog of your dreams, and soon you'll be bringing him home. Maybe you need to wait a couple of weeks until your purebred puppy is old enough to leave his mom and littermates . . . or only until tomorrow, when you get a final thumbs-up from the shelter or rescue group for the adult dog you want to adopt. Either way, you've got some time to kill between now and when your four-legged friend joins your household. That's time you could spend getting the stuff your canine companion will need.

Sure, you could wait till you've got Fido in tow to stop off at your local pet superstore and stock up on dog gear. But do you really want to be dashing madly up and down the aisles, throwing products willy-nilly into your shopping cart while also trying to manage an overexcited pooch? Better to make the most of your waiting time now: Stock up on the stuff that your dog will need to feel truly at home.

What should that gear include? Here's what every new dog should have:

A crate. Whether it's made of plastic or metal, a crate provides a secure place that a dog can call his own for resting, sleeping, or just plain retreating. When it comes to crates, material is less important than size. Any crate you choose must be big enough for your dog to stand up and turn around in, but not so large that he can pee at one end and sleep at the other.

Two dishes. Experts and experienced dog owners opt for two stainless steel dishes—one for food, the other for water—because they're dishwasher-safe and impervious to the ravages of puppy teeth.

Stock up on dog gear before your new pooch comes home.

A week's supply of dog food. Chapter nine of this book offers a detailed description of the many types of dog food available and analyzes the pros and cons of creating your own canine cuisine. For now, though, it's best to find out what the shelter, foster home, or breeder has been feeding your four-legged friend and lay in a small stash of the same food. Later, you can switch to another brand—or start making your dog's food yourself.

A collar. Every dog needs a collar to hold an identification tag, a rabies inoculation tag, and a license tag—not to mention the leash that keeps the two of you tethered in public. Stores offer plenty of collar styles to choose from, but most experts opt for either a soft nylon or thin leather buckle collar. A newcomer to the collar market is the breakaway collar. This nylon doodad releases if it accidentally becomes caught on a crate, fence, or canine playmate's teeth, thus eliminating the possibility of a collar accident.

A leash. Maybe Timmy never walked Lassie on a leash, but if you plan to take your dog anywhere in public, the two of you will need one. Your best bet is a six-foot leather leash. True, nylon or cotton leashes are cheaper—but if your dog pulls and the leash crosses your hand, the cheaper leash could leave a nasty abrasion on your palm. Leather is easier on the hands, and it lasts longer, too.

Grooming gear. Depending on the type of coat your dog has, you'll need at least one brush, a small pair of scissors, and a pair of nail clippers. Longhaired dogs also need combs. Chapter ten describes in detail the types of combs, brushes, and other grooming gear that are available and also which gear should be used for which coats. Other canine grooming necessities include shampoo, a soft toothbrush, and a tube of toothpaste made especially for dogs (toothpaste for people can upset a dog's stomach).

**SEVEN ITEMS YOUR NEW DOG
CAN'T DO WITHOUT**

- Crate
- Dishes
- Food
- Collar
- Leash
- Grooming gear
- Seat belt

Seat belt. Just as people need seat belts to improve their odds of surviving a car crash, so does your dog. Doggie seat belts work in conjunction with your car's seat belt system to provide your dog with the same protection that you get whenever you buckle up.

If you want to pamper your new pooch, here are some additional items to put on your pre-puppy shopping list:

A crate pad. A crate-sized foam mattress will make your dog's den that much more attractive to him—a big plus when you're housetraining him. Until he's mastered proper potty protocol, though, it's a good idea to use a waterproof mattress and covering.

A bed. Once your pooch is potty-trained, he won't need to use his crate so often (although he might want to). When that happens— or if your new canine companion is a shelter or rescue animal who's already housetrained—you can treat him to a comfortable bed of his very own. Many dogs like cuddler beds (also known as nests). These beds are made from foam rubber and include an extra layer of padding—kind of like a human bed's headboard— around the back. The extra padding helps the dog to feel more secure, because as he curls up and sleeps, he is protected from behind. Other dogs prefer pillows or cushions that let them stretch out and relax.

Canine clothing. Think your dog's fur protects him against the cold and rain? Maybe so—but then again, it can be awfully nice for a dog to emerge from a rainstorm without being dripping wet. The same is true when dealing with the cold; it's a lot easier for your pooch to potty outside in freezing weather if he's wearing some protection from the elements. For that reason, you might want to consider getting some apparel for your dog, especially if he's small and/or shorthaired.

A few toys. Most dogs love toys of some sort—but you may need to experiment to determine which playthings your particular pooch prefers. Some toys to avoid include those with parts that are small enough to swallow, those that your dog's teeth can destroy easily, and those that resemble real-life objects (e.g., shoes) that you don't want your dog to chew on.

A few treats. Just as you enjoy a culinary goodie every now and then, so too does your dog. Moreover, treats offer your pooch a great incentive to learn basic commands, such as coming when called and sitting when told. Chapter nine discusses the ins and outs of dog treats.

Baby gates. This nice-to-have item is sold in both pet stores and stores for human children—and for good reason: Both human and canine babies sometimes need to be kept away from certain areas of the house (for example, the top of a staircase) so that they don't hurt themselves or otherwise get into trouble. Consider investing in a hardware gate that swings open, rather than a pressure gate that you have to hop over. The latter is cheaper but can become a major irritant if you have to hop over it very often. And, if one of those hops ends up with you tumbling to the floor, the irritation could be replaced by real pain. Make sure, too, that you buy a gate with a mesh screen. They're safer than gates with bars; a puppy or a dog's head can get trapped between the bars.

Puppy playpen. Also known as an exercise pen (or ex-pen for short), this device looks a lot like a wire crate, except that it lacks a top and bottom. Its purpose is the same as that of a child's playpen: to give a puppy room to move around—but within a confined area so that he doesn't get into trouble. An ex-pen is great for puppies whose people are away during the day, as well as for pooches who, for some reason, can't get used to crates.

Where can you find all this canine paraphernalia? A pet superstore is an obvious option, but not the only one. A World Wide Web search for on-line pet retailers will yield scores of outlets that not only allow you to buy your gear on-line but often also send printed catalogs to their customers. And if you're in the market for a baby gate, you can expand your source pool to baby supply stores.

THE JOYS OF CRATING

I don't want to get my dog a crate; I think they look like little cages. And they seem cruel, as though you're putting a dog in prison. Why should I get one?

Your reaction to crates illustrates a big difference between people and dogs. Crates do look confining to most people. But to a dog, it can be an invitation to revisit his roots. That's because a crate is to a dog what a den is to a wolf. Canines of all kinds —domesticated or wild—each want to have a little place to call their own. This place, or den, is the place where the animal goes to rest, to sleep, and to feel safe.

For example, my dog, Cory, detests the household vacuum cleaner. He hates the noise it makes and the fact that it sucks up every little thing in its path. (Maybe he's afraid that the big machine will suck *him* up.) Whenever he sees me pull out that big black sucking machine, he barks frantically and tries to attack it—unless I put him in his crate. If I do, he simply waits quietly. Vacuuming my house is a lot less stressful for both Cory and me when he is safely ensconced in his crate.

A crate is also a priceless tool for housetraining your dog. The reason: wolves and dogs will do just about anything to avoid soiling their dens. Thus, by confining your dog to his special den—the crate—under carefully supervised conditions, you help him control his urge to potty at random. Instead, he learns to confine his bathroom maneuvers to the times and places that you specify. (More on this principle appears in chapter fourteen.)

Finally, if you and your dog ever have to travel together by plane, your dog needs to be able to stay in a crate. That's because airlines re-

quire people to place their dogs in regulation crates for the duration of
any airline flight. If your dog already feels comfortable in a crate, an
airplane trip will be much less stressful for him. The same principle
also applies to long car trips; a crated dog often is a much more comfortable interstate auto passenger than his safety-belted canine counterpart is.

PLASTIC OR METAL?

Which is better: a plastic crate or a metal crate?

It's really a matter of individual preference. Some people like plastic
crates because they're enclosed on three sides (except for the vents, of
course), which makes them more like the cozy, dark dens that many
dogs prefer. Another plus is that plastic crates can be used for airline
travel, while metal crates aren't permitted. A third advantage to plastic crates is that they generally cost less than metal crates do.

The big downside with plastic crates is that they can be cumber-
some. Unlike metal crates, plastic crates aren't collapsible. Instead,
they come in two molded halves. Although those halves can be nested
together, they still take up a lot of space. Another drawback is the fact
that dogs can chew plastic crates, while metal crates are impervious to
the chomping of canine choppers.

Metal crates offer collapsibility, which means that they can be
stashed away in small places when they're not being used. And because they're open all around, your dog can see what's going on in the
world even if he's confined to his den. This openness also offers more
ventilation, which can be an important advantage if your dog has any
breathing difficulties, which is often the case with short-nosed breeds
like bulldogs and pugs.

The bottom line here is that there is no bottom line. Assess your individual situation and your own special dog to decide who wins your
particular plastic-versus-metal sweepstakes.

ONE SIZE-FITS-ALL CRATE

My puppy is going to grow up to be a big dog, but I don't want to have to get a new crate for her every couple of weeks to fit her new size. Is there a crate that grows along with her?

Happily, the answer to your question is yes. The only catch is that you need to create such a crate yourself.

Here's how to do it: First, buy a plastic crate that will accommodate your puppy's adult size. Then make a divider: a barrier that will wall off part of the crate and can be adjusted as your puppy grows. It works the same way that the plate at the back of a file cabinet drawer does: You slide the divider back as your little one grows and needs more room.

To create the divider, get a piece of cardboard that's just a tad wider than the back of your puppy's new plastic crate. Place the cardboard inside the crate, inserting the sides of the cardboard into the ventilation slots on the sides of the crate. You may need to punch holes into the cardboard and use some wire to help fasten the divider to the crate. As your puppy grows, you can move the divider back to accommodate her changing size. And when she reaches her adult size, you can chuck the divider completely.

RETRACTABLE LEASH PROS AND CONS

I'd like my dog to have a little more freedom on our walks than a six-foot leash allows. Should I get a retractable leash?

Lots of dog people swear by retractable leashes: wires as long as thirty feet that clip to the dog's collar at one end and retract into a plastic container at the other. Retractable leash advocates feel that these devices give their pooches almost as much room to run around as they'd have if they were off leash, even though the dogs are still under their handlers' control.

These people have a point, but I'm not a big fan of retractable leashes. For one thing, the leash handle is hard to grip and can be uncomfortable to hold. A dog can easily jerk the entire apparatus out of your hand if he suddenly decides to take off after something—or someone. Moreover, some professional trainers believe that a dog who's walked with a retractable leash has a tougher time learning to walk nicely with a person than the dog who is walked with a regular leash.

Another problem with retractable leashes is that other people find it difficult to see the leash itself. I'm not the only person who's walked between a person and his dog and found myself tripping over the nearly invisible cord of a retractable leash.

Finally, using a retractable leash can cause you and your pooch to run afoul of local laws. That's because many municipalities stipulate that dog leashes should extend no more than six to ten feet. Consequently, if your dog's retractable leash is extended to its thirty-foot max, you're leaving yourself open to legal trouble—especially if someone sustains an injury after having tripped over that leash.

If you still want to give your dog more room to maneuver, go ahead and get the retractable leash—but use it with caution. And to teach your pooch to walk politely with you, shell out a few extra bucks to get him a regular leash, too.

SEAT BELT SAVVY

*Do I really need to get a seat belt for my dog? Half the time
I don't wear mine!*

Well, you should! In just about every U.S. jurisdiction, seat belts are required by law—for people, anyway. And for good reason: They save lives, either by themselves or in conjunction with an air bag system. The converse isn't necessarily true, though: An air bag working alone can be dangerous, even lethal, to an unbelted passenger.

But I digress. The objective behind buying doggie seat belts is to keep both you and your canine passenger safe in a car crash. Even a sudden stop can send an unsecured pooch catapulting all over the car, injuring both him and anyone else that he catapults into, and causing a serious accident to occur. And even if you don't have an accident, you don't want to have a dog climbing all over you while you're trying to drive.

These are safety concerns that some car manufacturers are starting to address. For example, in early 2002, both General Motors and Saab offered cars designed for the dog-owning motorist. The GM car, the GMC Envoy, featured an integrated safety belt and lots of other bells and whistles designed to get doggie and driver on their way safely and comfortably. The Saab 9-5 wagon included what the company called a trademarked pet safety belt as well as a panoply of other pet travel accessories.

But if you don't want to shell out five figures—or take on a hefty loan—to buckle Bowser up, it's perfectly fine to head to a local pet product retailer and pick a seat belt or harness that you can use in your current chariot. These devices are sized to fit your canine companion and cost well under $20.00. That's a small price to pay to ensure the safety of all your auto passengers, human and canine.

THE TRUTH ABOUT TRAINING COLLARS

I'm going to need to train my dog to walk nicely next to me while he's on the leash. So shouldn't I get him a training collar, rather than a plain old buckle collar?

In a word: no.

Many dog trainers believe that the term *training collar* is misleading. That's because such collars are designed to tighten uncomfortably around a dog's neck when the human dog-walker pulls on the leash. Consequently, many experts (myself included) prefer to tell it like it is when it comes to training collars: They are more accurately called *choke chains*.

Choke chains are difficult to use correctly—and when they're used incorrectly, they can damage a dog's windpipe. They also can literally shave the hair off the neck of a longhaired dog. Moreover, they often don't work: Many dogs who are subjected to these collars continue to pull their owners around as though they are in training for the *Ben Hur* chariot race. Finally, choke chains can be a real hazard if used as a regular collar. The dangling end of the collar can become caught on a crate, fence, or gate, resulting in the dog being strangled.

Chapter thirteen outlines better ways to teach your leashed dog good walking manners. Many a dog does just fine with a regular collar and leash, as long as there's a knowledgeable human walking with him. For dogs with walking issues, humane devices such as head halters can solve problems without causing the dog discomfort.

MEASURING UP

How can I tell what size collar to get my dog?

This one's easy: Take a tape measure, encircle your dog's neck, and jot down the result. Then add two inches. For example, if the dog's neck measures sixteen inches around, you'd need an eighteen-inch collar for her.

Once your dog has her pretty new collar, perform a simple test to make sure that it fits her properly. Do this by trying to slip two of your fingers between the collar and your dog's neck. If you can do this easily, you've got a collar that fits; if two fingers fit too snugly (or if you can fit only one finger) the collar is too tight. If you can slip in a third finger, the collar is too loose.

BED BASICS

The dog I'm getting is already housetrained, so I'm not getting him a crate. What kind of bed should I look for?

First, getting a crate can be a good idea even if your canine companion has already mastered his bathroom basics. The denning instinct doesn't die just because a dog has learned where and when to do his business.

Still, dogs enjoy their creature comforts as much as anyone else. That is reason enough to buy the potty-trained pooch his very own bed. And you'll find lots of beds to choose from: pillows/cushions, cuddler beds (also known as nests), beanbag beds, heated beds, and raised hammock-type beds. As you get to know your dog, you'll undoubtedly discover that he has certain sleeping preferences: Some dogs like to stretch out, others like to curl up, while still others like to do both.

For now, realize that the bed you choose today may not be the bed your dog will want to stick with. Probably the most versatile bed you can get him at the moment is a pillow or cushion-type bed that's big enough for him to stretch out on but allows him to curl up, too.

No matter what bed you choose, make sure it's big enough to accommodate your canine companion's sprawled-out size. And consider how you'll care for the bed, too; look for one that has a machine-washable zip-off cover. That way, your dog's bed will stay as fresh as yours does.

DISHING ABOUT DISHES

I don't want to get stainless steel dishes because I can't use them in the microwave to warm up my dog's food (I hear that dogs like their food warmed). Why shouldn't I get plastic or ceramic dishes?

Unfortunately, plastic dishes aren't always very good for dogs. Prolonged use has been known to cause some pooches to lose the pigment from their noses. But some ceramic dishes are just fine. They do indeed withstand the microwave better than stainless steel does; the latter can short out your microwave or at least produce an unwanted light show.

However, not all ceramic dishes are created equal. Imported dishes may contain lead, which could be potentially harmful to your four-legged friend. Check any ceramic dish to see if it's made in the U.S.A. If it is, and you like it, go ahead and buy it.

PLAYING IT SAFE WITH TOYS

I want to pick toys that I know my dog will like but that are also safe for him. What kinds of toys should I get?

Alas, there's no way to know in advance what kind of toy your dog will go for. The fact that your dog is a Labrador retriever doesn't guarantee that he'll want to retrieve the tennis balls you throw. I know this from experience: My own dog, Cory, has a basket full of toys that I thought he'd love—but that he took one look at and never bothered with again.

You can, however, pick toys that are safe for your dog to play with. Here are some guidelines for picking the right playthings for pooch:

Know that size matters. A dog's size is probably the most important factor in determining whether a toy is right for him to use. For example, you wouldn't give a tiny three-inch chew toy to a Saint Bernard; the toy could end up in his windpipe.

Choose toys meant for dogs. Yes, we all know that dogs and puppies love to play with people's socks. But unless you want to have a whole bunch of torn, mismatched socks—or worse, a sock that ends up obstructing your dog's intestinal tract (which would require emergency surgery)—stick with products that dogs are meant to play with.

Get to know your dog. Hold off on getting most toys until you know a little bit more about your canine companion. For example, if he turns out to be a chewer, you're not going to want to get him a soft plush toy that he can destroy in five minutes. The same is true with a squeak toy—unless you want to end up at the animal hospital with your vet palpating the dog's stomach to see if the squeaker is there.

HOW TO FIND A VETERINARIAN

There's something else you need to find for your dog before you bring him home, but you're not likely to find that something in the same place you acquire the crate, collar, leash, and other paraphernalia. That something is actually some*one*: a veterinarian.

Why do you need a vet before you bring Fido home? Because within a day of Fido's arrival, you'll need to take him to a veterinarian for his first checkup. In fact, many contracts from breeders, rescue groups, and animal shelters require new pooch parents to bring their four-legged friends to a vet for a checkup within forty-eight hours of adoption. That's why it's good to know beforehand exactly who you'll have look at your new canine companion.

Start by getting the names of a few veterinarians in your area. A good place to start is with the human guardians of dogs already in your neighborhood. You can also check in the phone book, with local breed or kennel clubs, or on-line at websites such as that for the American Animal Hospital Association (www.healthypet.com). Such sites often have animal hospital locators that can help you find accredited facilities that are within easy driving distance.

Once you've identified a couple of possibilities, pay each a visit. During the visit, you can get answers to the following questions:

What are the office hours? If you're away from home during the day, a veterinary practice that's open only from 9 till 5 won't be very convenient for you. Look for a practice that operates at hours that are compatible with your schedule.

How do you pay for services? A practice that accepts credit cards can be a godsend if, for example, you bring your dog in for an emergency that becomes unexpectedly pricey. A case in point: When my dog, Cory, needed to have a sock removed from his stomach, the bill for the evaluation and emergency surgery came to more than $1,000. We'd have been in trouble if the vet hadn't been willing to take plastic.

What's the hospital like? An animal hospital should be clean and orderly, without any noxious odors. The hospital staff—from front desk to kennel attendant, not to mention the veterinarians them-selves—should be courteous, customer-oriented, and display a caring attitude toward their animal patients.

Is the hospital close to your home? You're more likely to be consci-entious about your canine companion's care if his doctor is a ten-minute drive away, rather than an hour.

Are there backup systems? Find out what procedures are in place if your dog has a medical emergency after hours. Is there a vet-erinarian on call? Is there an emergency clinic that you can be referred to?

Can you get appointments quickly? If getting an appointment takes a wait of more than a few days, the practice may too busy (or too understaffed) to accommodate the needs of you and your dog. The same may be true if people and pets spend a lot of time cooling their heels in the waiting room before a veterinarian can see them.

CHAPTER 5

Getting Your Home Ready for Your New Dog

YOU'VE TAKEN ADVANTAGE of some pre-pooch time and stocked up on all the gear you think your canine companion-to-be could possibly need: crate, dishes, food, collar, leash, and more. The result, you think, is the transformation of your home for people into a puppy palace—or, if your new arrival is older, an ideal doggie den. You're sure that now, finally, you're ready for your brand-new dog to cross your threshold and take his place in front of your hearth.

Well, I hate to disappoint you—but you've still got a ways to go. It takes more than buying a bundle of dog equipment to be ready for your new four-legged friend. You also need to make sure that your home is ready.

Think about it. The parents of new human children spend not only money, but time, setting up their little one's nursery. They contemplate exactly where in the house that nursery will be. And once they pick the room, they probably spend a few more hours figuring out exactly where the crib, changing table, dresser drawers, rocking chair, and other accoutrements of babyhood will be placed (I know I did!).

Happily, your new dog doesn't need to have an entire room dedicated to his comfort. In fact, if he is confined to one room of your home, he'll be very unhappy—as I explain in chapters eight and twelve. However, a dog does require a home that takes his needs into account.

Getting basic dog supplies is a good start toward achieving that goal. Once you've stocked up on all that dog gear, designing a dog-friendly home is simply a matter of putting the gear into the right places and getting the hazardous stuff in your house beyond your new dog's reach.

Your first consideration in designing your new dog's personal paradise is to figure out exactly how he will fit into your home. Specifically, where do you want him to eat, sleep, and otherwise spend his time?

For most people, the best place to install a canine eatery is in a corner of their kitchen. That's the place where you're most likely to store the dog food, and the floor there is easier to clean than anywhere else in the house. The kitchen's also where the microwave is, making a quick warm-up of your dog's dinner fast and convenient, and where the dishwasher is—which leaves you no excuse for neglecting to wash your dog's dishes every day.

A kitchen-based canine dining area also has some pluses from your dog's point of view. The biggest of these advantages is that the kitchen is often the heart of the action and activity in a human household. Your dog, being the social creature that he is, will appreciate being able to eat in close proximity to that activity. However, by putting his dishes in the corner of the kitchen, he'll get that proximity without getting himself stepped on or tripped over.

As for sleeping, it's my firm opinion that the best place for your pooch to slumber is with at least one of his people—in other words, in a bedroom. Why? Mainly because it gives the dog and his human companion(s) a chance to be together for an extended period of time every day (or, rather, night). Even if they're not doing anything other than snoozing, that time together builds the bond between them. Your social dog craves this time with you—the more he has, the better your relationship with him will be.

And what if you are, ahem, doing something other than snoozing? To put it bluntly, can your dog stick around if you and your spouse or significant other engage in the act of love?

The answer is a resounding yes. Dogs are very discreet. Unlike human beings, they do not go blabbing to their friends and acquaintances about what goes on in the boudoir. In fact, when it comes to human bedroom activities, many dogs sleep through the entire proceeding. In any case, though, the value to a dog of sleeping in the same room as one's humans far outweighs any squeamishness that the humans may have over the prospect.

One more thing: The in-bedroom sleep is particularly valuable for new puppies, who often feel lost and lonely without their littermates— and who also need to have a responsible human nearby to help them if they have to go potty in the middle of the night. If you are your puppy's roommate, you're much more likely to hear her whimper if she needs a midnight bathroom break than if she's stuck alone in the kitchen or basement.

And speaking of bathroom breaks, you also need to decide where your dog's potty will be. If your new canine companion is a teeny-tiny dog (such as a Lhaso apso, shih tzu, Chihuahua, or other toy breed), and/or if you have limited access to the outdoors, you might want to consider setting up an indoor bathroom of either newspapers or a doggie litter box. Otherwise, check around your backyard to determine the best place for your pooch to potty. An ideal outdoor potty spot is an area that's near your house (so that you and your dog don't have to go too far to get to his bathroom) and is easy to clean up.

If you live in a city and your dog is too big to use a litter box, look for an area that's easy to clean up and, if you have a puppy younger

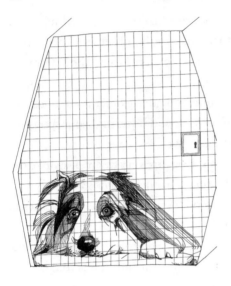

A crate is one place your dog
can feel safe and secure.

than sixteen weeks of age, isn't frequented by other dogs. That's because young puppies aren't fully immunized against serious diseases
such as distemper and parvovirus until they're sixteen weeks old.
Consequently, it's crucial for you to keep your little one from being exposed to these diseases until his fortified immune system can take over
the job. More on choosing a potty spot—and everything else you ever
wanted to know about housetraining—appears in chapter fourteen.

Finally, where do you want your dog to be at those times when he's
not eating or sleeping, but you're not around to supervise him? If your
answer to that question is "Anywhere he wants," you may be in for an
unwelcome surprise. A new puppy or new dog who's immediately
allowed to have full run of his new home often makes a mess of that
home by making bathroom boo-boos and/or chewing through your
carpets, walls, and upholstery.

Chapters eight and fourteen deal in detail with how to help your
dog cope with the emotional issues, potty problems, and everyday
doggie instincts that all too often wreak havoc on a home's decor, not
to mention the bond between that home's human and canine resi-

dents. But for now, you should plan on instituting some sort of confinement for your dog to keep him and your home safe during those times when you can't be with him—at least for the first few weeks.

A crate is a good start, because it offers your dog the cozy den he needs to feel safe and secure. However, safety and security will give way to crate hatred, not to mention accidents, if he's warehoused in the crate all day. A better option is to use baby gates, a puppy playpen, or even doors to confine your four-legged friend to an easily cleaned area, such as your kitchen or laundry room when you can't be around.

Making your house a dog-friendly home isn't difficult—it just takes a little bit of planning and forethought. The following questions and answers will further help you turn your domicile into a castle that's fit for men, women, and dogs.

DOING THE DOO

I know my puppy's going to have at least a few bathroom accidents before I get her housetrained. What's the best way to clean up those accidents?

Congratulations on your pragmatic approach to puppy parenting! You're absolutely right to be concerned about cleaning up your little darling's toileting transgressions. That's because canine waste is to dogs as a magnet is to metal: In both instances, the pull is irresistible.

If your four-legged friend takes a whiz on your carpet, and the resulting puddle is not cleaned up quickly and completely, he will—I promise!—come back to reanoint that puddle spot over and over again. The same is true if he decides to take a dump on the same carpet. To keep your canine companion from making either of these unwelcome deposits, it's crucial that you do more than physically remove any puppy puddle, pile, and resulting stain. You also must remove any and all odors that emanate from any such deposit.

To do that, make sure that the label of any cleaning product you use clearly states that it will remove pet stains and odor. Such products are armed with special enzymes that not only absorb a stain but also defuse any lingering fragrance. Consequently, the dog can't smell the scene of his crime—and thus, isn't drawn back to the scene to repeat his transgression. You can find these products at any good pet supply store, in pet product catalogs, or at most pet supply websites. Look for brands like Nature's Miracle, Simple Solution, or Anti-Icky-Poo (yes, that's actually the name of a product). Then, be sure to follow the manufacturers' directions.

Unfortunately, there are no shortcuts or alternatives to using a commercial enzymatic pet stain cleaner. For example, ammonia—although it's contained in many perfectly good household cleaning products—is absolutely the wrong thing to use when cleaning up a canine bathroom mishap. That's because ammonia smells like urine to dogs. Consequently, the odor from a spot cleaned with ammonia will simply encourage your dog to come back and rechristen it.

And no matter what you've heard about using club soda to clean up canine bathroom boo-boos, forget it. Yes, it's cheaper and available at more places than commercial pet stain cleaners are. But—and it's a big but—the soda removes only the stain, not the odor. Thus, you may not see the stain, but your dog will smell what you can't see. And once he smells it, you can count on him coming back to perform an encore on the very spot you worked so hard to clean.

HAIRY PROBLEMS

Our new dog is part golden retriever. Although he's beautiful and we can't wait till he comes home, I'm worried about all the dog hair that I know will soon be shed all over my house. How do I clean it up— or, better still, keep him from shedding in the first place?

As the dog-mama of a gorgeous long-coated Sheltie, I sympathize with your cleaning quandary. Longhaired dogs are lovely to look at, but when that long hair is shed, the homes such dogs live in look decidedly unlovely.

Frequent vacuuming of your carpets and upholstery (at least once a week) can go a long way toward keeping your home's bad dog hair days to a minimum. Change the vacuum cleaner bag frequently, and use the top suction setting for whatever you're vacuuming. Of course, check the manufacturer's instructions for specific suggestions.

To clean bare floors, you can either use your vacuum's floor attachment and suck the errant hair up, or you can opt to use an electrostatic dry sweeper. These handy little cloths use static electricity to pull dust, hair, crumbs, and other household debris off floors and furniture. They're sold in most supermarkets under trade names such as Swiffer (manufactured by Procter & Gamble) and Grab It (manufactured by S. C. Johnson). The cloth is wound around a special mop. Wield the mop over your floors, and you'll be amazed at how much hair and dirt come up. And it's a lot quicker to use than hauling out a heavy vacuum cleaner and fiddling with the machine's floor attachment.

But perhaps the best way to minimize shedding is to get the hair off your longhaired dog before he sheds it. Do this with thorough, frequent brushings: not just a cursory pat on the back but a complete, down-to-the-skin brushing over his entire body. I brush my Sheltie, Cory, a couple of times a week with a metal pin brush and comb. The entire job, from head to tail, takes about thirty minutes. Bigger dogs take longer, smaller dogs take less time.

You can also take steps to direct where some of the hair will go. For example, if you don't want Fifi to shed on the living room sofa, don't let her up on that sofa in the first place. If, despite your prohibitions, she refuses to stay away from the sofa, close off the room or find some other way to limit her access to the forbidden furniture.

Finally, if you're wearing your sexiest black dress or a just-rented tux, try not to give your light-colored dog a hug before you go out on the town. That suggestion may seem obvious—but I've made just that mistake with Cory before departing for an evening's merriment. He probably enjoyed the hug, but my dress sported some unwelcome white Sheltie hair as a result. For such sartorial emergencies, a lint brush or roller is indispensable.

THE ART OF DOG-PROOFING

I'm worried about my new puppy getting into trouble in my house: things like falling down the stairs, overturning wastebaskets, chewing on electrical cords, and drinking out of the toilet. How can I keep him from doing these things without watching him every single second?

Puppy parents and human parents have a lot in common—including worries about household hazards. Parents of human children respond to these worries by childproofing their homes before those children become mobile. Childproofing, for the uninitiated, is taking any and all possible steps to eliminate common domestic dangers, such as dangling electrical cords, easily opened cabinets that contain toxic household cleaners, toilet seats that lift and allow children to sample the water inside, and open electrical outlets.

At least the parents of human children have a few months between the infant's birth and his discovery of crawling to complete their childproofing. But while inquisitive puppies are in just as much danger from these and other household hazards, their human guardians have no such temporal luxury. When puppies come home, they're already mobile and ready to get into anything. Consequently, the prudent guardian puppy-proofs his home before the pup joins the household—or, failing that, as soon as humanly possible after the pup arrives. Here are some steps to take to puppy-proof your domicile:

Get down on all fours. Yes, really. Crawl around your home so that you can get a pup's eye view of what will attract his attention— and what will get him into trouble.

Tack down electrical cords. If allowed to dangle, electrical cords could prove all too tempting to a puppy who wants to paw at them—or worse, chew on them. Fasten them to the floor or wall with duct tape.

Block off staircases. An unexpected tumble down the stairs can be just as harmful to a puppy as to a human baby. Wherever possible, close the doors that lead to staircases; place baby gates at both ends of any others.

Keep cabinets shut. To keep your curious canine out of any cabinets that contain household cleansers or other dangerous (to him) substances, install door guards on the inside doors. These door guards are available at any toy or baby supply store.

Ditto for toilet lids. Although canine drinking from the toilet provokes considerable laughter among those canines' people, an open toilet could be a drowning pool for a puppy who manages to worm his way into one. Keep the toilet seat down at all times (this suggestion includes you, gentlemen!).

Take out trash. Empty your wastebaskets often, and keep the doors to the rooms they're located in closed until you do. The same goes for garbage cans; empty them often, and keep the lids closed in between emptyings. (Special note for women: Many dogs can't resist the scent of discarded feminine products! Wrap used maxi-pads and panti-liners securely with toilet paper before stashing them in the trash. Do the same with used tampon inserters.)

In addition to taking the above steps, however, any new puppy guardian needs to be vigilant. Watch your little darling closely while he explores his new home. If you can't watch him, place him someplace where you know he'll be safe—like in his crate.

SLEEPING WITH THE KIDS

My kids want our new puppy to sleep in their room. Is this a good idea?

Probably not—at least not right away. A new puppy is likely to have some restless nights when he first comes to live with you and your family. For one thing, he may be lonesome for his mama and littermates, and he probably will express that loneliness with whining and crying. Because you, the adult, are likely to be doing most of the puppy care, that puppy is going to look to you for comfort. If you're sleeping elsewhere, you can't give it to him.

And if your puppy needs a middle-of-the-night bathroom break (which is likely if he's under four months of age), you need to be there to make sure he gets it.

That's not to say that Fido can't bunk down with your offspring when they're all a little older. In fact, my dog, Cory, sleeps in my thirteen-year-old daughter's bedroom at night. However, they didn't start their nightly slumber parties until Cory was fully housetrained and almost fully grown. And even now, he sleeps in the master bedroom with my husband and me if he's recovering from an illness, or if my daughter is away.

SLEEPING ON THE BED

I'm single. Is there any reason that my dog shouldn't be able to sleep on my bed with me?

It does feel nice, especially on a cold night, to have a bundle of canine warmth and fur cuddling up next to you. But having your dog sleep on your bed is probably not a good idea—at least not when he first comes to live with you. For one thing, if your new arrival is a puppy, he's likely to be injured if you roll over on him in your sleep. But even if he's a bigger guy, sharing a bed with Fido can create confusion that may jeopardize the good start you want for your relationship with him.

That's because your objective in those first few days is to become someone whom your dog, that quintessential pack animal, considers to be a benevolent leader of his pack. It doesn't matter whether your pack consists of two or twenty-two members; your canine companion is looking to see who's at the top of the hierarchy and who's at the bottom. Ideally—from both his viewpoint and yours—you are the top dog in his pack.

Unfortunately, sleeping in your bed may give your dog the mistaken impression that he is equal to you in status. A dog who's unsure of his status is often a dog with behavioral problems such as aggressiveness, hyperactivity, or other antisocial issues.

Once you and your four-legged friend have established your respective places in your pack, you may find that sharing your bed with him has no effect on that hierarchy. If so, go ahead and invite him up—but only when you feel sure that he thoroughly understands and accepts his place in the scheme of things.

THE TOXIC NINE

You may adore your lush, green *Ficus benjamina* (weeping fig) tree, but you know enough not to eat it. Alas, a dog has no such knowledge. If his canine curiosity prompts him to taste your tree, the consequences could be deadly. And of course, the weeping fig is not the only common indoor plant that is toxic to dogs. Here are some others:

Asparagus fern	Marijuana
Dumb cane	Mistletoe
Dieffenbachia	Philodendron (most varieties)
Eucalyptus	Pothos (most varieties)

Beyond the "Toxic Nine" are other household hazards, such as that great human comfort food, chocolate, as well as antifreeze, rat poison, household garbage, onions, and pennies.

It's crucial to keep your curious canine away from these substances—either by not having them in the house at all, or by putting
them in places that you're absolutely sure are beyond your dog's reach.

If, despite all your efforts, you discover your four-legged friend par-
taking of any of these plants, bring him to your veterinarian immediately. And to help your vet help your pooch quickly, put in a call to the
ASPCA Animal Poison Control Center in Urbana, Illinois. The center is
staffed by veterinary toxicologists who know exactly the right antidote
for the poison your pooch ingested. A consultative call costs $45 (have
your credit card on hand when you call), which is a small investment to
make in order to save your dog's life.

The center's phone number is 1-888-426-4435. More information
on keeping pets safe from poison is available at the center's website:
www.apcc.aspca.org.

CHAPTER 6

Starting Life with Your New Dog

ETTING YOUR NEW dog's life with you off to a good start is a matter of both being prepared and not expecting too much too soon. You've already got much of the preparation covered: You've stocked up on dog gear and gotten your house ready for the arrival of your new canine companion. There's just one more thing you need to do: Get yourself ready.

Ironically, by getting yourself ready you'll also downplay your expectations of your new family member. That's because a big part of getting yourself ready is to try to think the way your dog does, rather than the usual way that a human being thinks. In other words, to get yourself ready for life with your dog, you need to put yourself in your dog's place.

If your new four-legged friend is a puppy, you need to understand what he's about to go through. Sure, he's embarking on life with you in a wonderful new home. But he isn't going to know that your home is so terrific—at least not right away. All he knows is that he suddenly is without his mama, his littermates, and the human caregivers he's known for his entire (admittedly short) life. Not surprisingly, he may be aloof, or confused, or even frightened of you, as he struggles to process what's happening to him. Or, conversely, he may be excited by all the changes he's experiencing. One thing is certain, though: He doesn't have a clue as to what this next phase of life holds in store for him.

On the other hand, if your new canine companion is a full-grown dog, he's probably not leaving the comforts of a home with a nurturing breeder. Instead, he may be departing from an animal shelter where—despite the good care he was given—he alternated between feeling bewildered at the noise and activity around him and feeling puzzled over the loss of his previous home. Alternatively, he may be a dog who was rescued from a less-than-ideal household and spent time in a foster home recovering from his ordeal. That foster home may have been the first time in a long time that your rescue dog has felt safe and secure—and to his way of thinking, that security is now being jeopardized by yet another change. Like the breeder's puppy, he doesn't know what's going to happen next.

You can help your dog face his future with confidence.

No matter where he comes from, adjusting to life with you—however wonderful you are—will be a stressful time for your new dog. You can help offset that stress by the way you treat him over the next few hours, days, and weeks. Starting with the car ride home, you can help your dog face his future with confidence and help him realize that life with you is going to be very, very good.

WHAT TO BRING FOR THE CAR RIDE HOME

What do we need to take in the car for when we bring our new dog home?

That first ride in the car with your new canine companion may leave you feeling as though you need to bring a U-Haul to accommodate all of his accessories and equipment. Rest assured that riding with your pooch won't always seem like such an expedition. But for that first trip in your vehicle, you'd do well to bring along the following items:

Leash and collar. If you need to make a pit stop on the way home, having your dog on leash will ensure that he stays safe and close to you.

Safety belt or crate. Just like any other passenger in your car, your new dog or puppy needs to be restrained while traveling—for your safety as well as for his. Unless he's large, you'll probably find it easier to put him in a crate, close the crate door, and secure the crate with a seat belt. Put the dog or crate in the front seat with you if you're traveling alone, but place the seat as far away from the dashboard as possible to guard against injury if the car's air bag deploys. If you have another person coming with you, place the dog or crate and the second person in the back seat.

Towels, sheets, and/or blankets. If you haven't already bought a mattress for the crate, line the bottom with some soft towels or a blanket so that it will be more comfortable for your dog to lie on.

For the dog who's secured with a safety belt, place some towels or a sheet on the seat where he'll be sitting. Have some extras on hand in case he has a potty accident or vomits while in the car.

Paper towels. A roll of paper towels will come in handy for cleaning up the aforementioned bathroom boo-boo or result of car-sickness.

One or two plastic bags. You'll need these to clean up any poop that your puppy deposits on the way home. Bread loaf bags and newspaper bags are ideal.

Chew toy. Having something to chew on can distract your new dog from any apprehension he feels when he leaves his old home and starts a new life with you.

STUFF FROM THE OLD HOME

What should the breeder, rescue person, or shelter volunteer give me when I pick up my new dog?

No matter where or from whom you adopt your new dog, you should get a contract that transfers ownership of your dog to you and specifies both your obligations and those of the individual or institution from whom you're acquiring the dog. You should also be given the animal's health record: written documentation of when he was born and/or arrived at the shelter or foster home and the veterinary care he has received, such as immunizations, spaying and neutering, deworming, and/or other procedures. A breeder or rescue volunteer may also give you a few days' supply of the food she's been feeding your puppy or dog.

And to get your puppy's housetraining off to a good start, consider asking his breeder for one more item: a sheet of paper toweling that's been scented with a bit of your pup's urine. This pretreated sheet will speed up your pooch's potty-training process.

PIT STOPS ON THE ROAD

It's going to take us an hour or so to bring our puppy from the breeder's to our home. Do we need to stop to let him go to the bathroom?

A midway pit stop is probably a good idea, particularly if you notice that your canine passenger is getting restless. Find a grassy place and pull over. Put a leash on your little one before you open the car door; then take him to the spot where you want him to do his business. To help your puppy figure out where that spot is, place the prescented paper towel that you got from his breeder on the spot where you want him to go.

If your puppy poops or pees, tell him in a high, soft voice what a good dog he is, and take a minute or two to pet him. Use a plastic bag to clean up any poop and deposit it in a trashcan or wastebasket.

After that, take your canine genius back to the spot to give him another chance to go. He may or may not do it, but you've at least given him a chance. Either way, you can then continue to your destination —and know that you and he have already started to form a lifelong bond.

WHAT HAPPENS ONCE WE GET HOME?

What should we do with our puppy or dog once we get him home?

As soon as you and your four-legged friend arrive home, take him to the outdoor bathroom area you've selected, or the indoor potty area you've prepared. Car rides often prompt a pooch to eliminate as soon as the ride has ended, so do this before you head into the house.

Once you've reached the designated potty spot, place the prescented cloth on the ground and let your pooch give it a sniff. When he pees or poops, praise him gently but enthusiastically, so that he knows he's done what you wanted him to do.

If he doesn't go, give him a couple of minutes to explore—but even if he does go, don't bring him into your home immediately. Many puppies (and even a few grown-up dogs) need to take multiple whizzes during a single bathroom break before their bladders are totally empty.

Once you're sure he's done, take your dog inside and let him explore your domicile for a little while. Keep an eye on him the entire time, though, to see if he needs to go again. Signs of an imminent deposit include a sudden halt to activity, intense sniffing, circling, and beginning to squat. If you see any such signs, get your dog back out to the potty spot he used before. The scent from his previous bathroom break will prompt him to repeat his performance. When he does, give him lots of praise.

After an hour or so of getting to know each other, put your new dog in his crate or other confined area and let him take a nap. Watch to see when he wakes up, though. When he does, whisk him to his bathroom area—and again, be sure to praise him when he goes.

CRATING 101

I don't think my new dog has ever seen the inside of a crate. How do I introduce him to one?

Some dogs don't have any idea that crates exist, while others need a little time to appreciate their virtues. And if you're not careful, a dog may end up considering the crate to be nothing less than a pooch penitentiary in which he's incarcerated. If your dog ends up viewing his crate in a negative light, housetraining him and traveling with him may become unnecessarily complicated.

The key word here is *unnecessarily.* That's because, with a careful introduction, your dog can learn to view his crate as the nifty doggie den that it's designed to be. Here's what to do to help your dog look on his crate as a refuge, rather than a prison:

Tie the door open. The key to successful crate introduction is to make it a gradual process and to eliminate any events that might spook your canine companion. One such event is the accidental closure or slamming of the crate door before your dog is fully accustomed to the crate. To prevent that closure, tie the door open —and leave it that way until your four-legged friend is going into the crate by himself.

Let him check out the crate. Allow your canine companion to walk around and sniff the crate. After a couple of minutes of exploration, put a treat or toy just inside the door. If he ventures inside the crate to retrieve the goodie, praise him; if he hesitates, encourage him to try in a high, happy, enthusiastic voice. Either way, let him decide when to venture inside—and when he does, tell him what a good boy he is.

Shut the door for a few seconds. When your puppy is consistently and willingly entering his crate, go to the next step: shutting the door momentarily. Put a treat inside the crate. When the dog enters, *quietly* shut the door, but leave it shut for no more than five seconds. After that, tell him what a good dog he is, open the door, and coax him out. Praise him again and give him another treat. Keep doing this, gradually increasing the time the door remains closed, until your four-legged friend stays calmly in the crate for five minutes or so.

Leave the room. Once your dog is able to spend five minutes in his crate without getting bent out of shape, move to the final step of Crating 101: leaving the room while the dog's in the crate. Lure him into the crate with either a safe chew toy or several treats (not just one). When he's in, shut the door quietly and leave the room —but only for a minute or so.

Come back and check. After that minute is up, come back into the room and check to see what your friend is doing. If he's content, leave again and come back in a few minutes. Keep checking until

he's finished his chewing or eating, or is showing signs of restlessness or distress. At that point, let him out of his crate and praise
him for his achievement. Keep this up until he's able to stay in his
crate for thirty minutes.

NIGHTTIME GOINGS-ON

*I've heard some real horror stories about the first few nights with a new
dog or puppy: that they whine, cry, yodel, and otherwise carry on so
much that their families can't get a decent night's sleep. Is this going
to happen when my new dog comes home—and if so, what can I
do about it?*

Put yourself in your pooch's place. If he's a puppy, this is his very first
night away from the place, people, and dogs with whom he's spent
his entire young life. He misses the smells, sights, and sounds that
he's grown up with. Making the switch from sharing a bed with one's
warm littermates to sleeping by oneself in a crate or other doggie bed
is difficult for some puppies to negotiate.

An adult dog may have some first-night jitters, too. She may be
wondering what's going to happen next after having endured one or
more moves to new homes, a shelter, and/or foster care.

When viewed from that perspective, you can deal with your new
dog's nighttime crying and other vocalizations with sympathy, not im-
patience. That same sympathy can also help you to keep those noctur-
nal cries and whispers to a minimum. Here's what you can do:

Let her in. Sure, it's tempting to put your dog's crate in the kitchen,
basement, or laundry room so that her nighttime concert doesn't
keep you awake. But being away from you, having to sleep all
alone, is likely to worsen your dog's distress. Show her some sympathy: Share your bedroom with her.

Keep her close. Put your dog's crate close to your bed. That way,
she can see you, smell you, and hear you breathe—all of which

will help reassure her that she's not alone, and that someone's there who can take care of her.

Keep your bed to yourself. You might think that bringing your canine companion up on your bed to snuggle with you will help calm her even more. And you're probably right. However, by inviting your dog up on your bed, you may open a Pandora's box of other problems. For one thing, she might have a bathroom accident on your bed. In addition, she might become confused as to who really is top dog in your pack.

Play some music. Some calm, soothing music—think classical or New Age, not rock or pop—can help your frightened friend settle herself and relax enough to get to sleep.

Use your hands. If, despite your efforts, your dog still fusses, lay your hand on her crate and tell her in a gentle but firm voice, "Fifi (or whatever her name is), go to sleep."

Have your shoes ready. If the two of you have been slumbering for a while, but you're awakened by your dog's whining or restlessness, she probably needs a bathroom break. Grab your shoes and her leash and take her outside to her potty area. Once she does her business, though, take her inside (after praising her, of course!) and put her back to bed—no 2:00 A.M. playing, unless you like frolicking at that hour.

Know this won't last. A new puppy or dog's nighttime cries usually don't last more than a night or two. After that, she'll probably sleep as soundly as you do, unless she's got to make a middle-of-the-night pit stop.

INTRODUCING OTHER ANIMALS

How should we introduce our new dog to our cat? How about to our guinea pig?

The fact that you are overjoyed to be welcoming a new puppy or dog to your family does not necessarily mean that your resident cat or other critter will share your delight. In fact, it's more likely that they will be less than thrilled at the addition to their family. You need to take this reality into account when introducing your new canine companion to the other nonhuman members of your household.

Different cats react in different ways to a dog's debut. To be on the safe side—and to show some respect for the fact that the cat was, after all, in your home first—make sure that the first dog–cat meeting occurs from opposite sides of the crate. In other words, place your new dog or puppy inside his crate or other enclosure, and let your kitty investigate the newcomer and his environs.

If the fur doesn't fly, and the hisses and barks are minimal, take the next step: Hold your dog on your lap (or, if he's too big, on leash and lying down next to you on the floor) and allow your cat to approach—or, more likely, to run away. Either way is fine, as long as nobody gets bitten or scratched. Continue to monitor the two animals until you're absolutely sure that they can coexist peacefully—or that one can get away from the other without any problems. If you're leaving the house or otherwise are in a situation where you can't supervise your dog and cat, separate them until you return.

Other animals such as guinea pigs generally spend most of their time in cages—and when your dog's around, that's where they need to stay. A dog has a strong instinct to chase and catch prey, which is what the guinea pig will look like to him. The result, alas, probably will be the guinea pig's demise.

CALMING DOWN THE KIDS

Our kids are just bouncing off the walls with excitement now that they finally have their new dog. I'm afraid that the dog will get spooked by all their commotion. What should I do?

You're right to be concerned. Overenthusiastic children can easily overwhelm a puppy or dog who already may be a little freaked by all the changes that suddenly are bombarding her. And if those children are under the age of six or so, their eagerness to cuddle and hug the new family member could end up hurting both them and the dog, because young children often can't gauge their own strength.

As a parent it's up to you to not only set limits but also to help your children empathize with your new canine companion. That's why it's a good idea to have a little family conference before the dog comes home. Explain to your children that the new puppy or dog may feel a little scared and that she needs for everyone to stay calm and give her some space. Then, set those limits: no screaming, shouting, or squealing; no roughhousing; gentle petting only.

And, to be on the safe side, don't leave kids under the age of six alone with your canine companion—ever. Even the gentlest dog can react with growl or nip when a small child pokes her in the eye or pulls at her tail. Under-sixes have a hard time realizing that Fido isn't a walking, barking stuffed toy, but instead is a living creature with feelings. They—and Fido—need your presence to ensure that all concerned stay out of harm's way.

INTRODUCING THE NEIGHBORS

The neighborhood kids (and their parents) want to welcome our new pooch to our block with a puppy party. We're glad that they're so happy to have our dog here, but is this really a good idea?

Well, no—at least not right away. Your new canine companion will probably be on sensory overload just from meeting you and the rest of your family during the first few days she's in your home. Being the guest of honor at a neighborhood bash might be more than she could handle. And if she's a puppy, she might look like prey, rather than a playmate, to the bigger dogs in the neighborhood—a mistake that could have dire consequences for your new arrival.

A better way to meet the neighbors—canine and otherwise—is to give your new dog a chance to chill for at least the first few days she's with you. Give her time to get used to you and your family and to settle in to her new domicile. Then, invite a few people at a time to meet her.

As for other dogs, it might be better for them to meet in neutral territory, such as a park, if your dog is an adult. That way, neither dog will be dealing with turf issues when they encounter each other. If your new pooch is under sixteen weeks of age, though, hold off on any meetings with other dogs until she's had all of her puppy shots.

THE NAME GAME

In what perhaps is his best-loved play, *Romeo and Juliet*, William Shakespeare appears to declare that names shouldn't be important. Speaking through Juliet, the Bard says that a name says little about the "dear perfection" of the individual the name refers to. However, when it comes to naming dogs and other pets, experts disagree with Shakespeare's contention.

Veterinarian Myrna Milani, who specializes in the study of the human–animal bond, says that a pet's name "sums up a lot about the expectations that the owner places on the relationship with the pet." Unfortunately, those expectations often say more about the owner than the pet.

For example, owners of intimidating-looking dogs such as Rottweilers or Dobermans often give them names that match those breeds' fearsome reputations. Such names can cause people to respond to such a dog in ways that in turn trigger unwelcome reactions from the animal. Other owners stick their canine companions with babyish or humorous monikers that a dog may find demeaning.

"The dog recognizes what's going on," says Brother Marc, one of the world-famous monks of New Skete who raise and train German shepherds. "You can see this in the hesitation of the dog to engage happily" with an owner who uses such a name. Put another way, the dog may recognize that he's being laughed at or otherwise demeaned, and may react unhappily.

To avoid these naming pitfalls, here are some suggestions:

Pick a name that says something about your pooch. Examples: Shadow for a black Lab, Saffron for a golden retriever.

Choose a name that's easy to learn. Most experts suggest limiting a name to one or two syllables. Such names take less time for a dog to recognize than a longer one does.

Pick a name your dog will grow into. A babyish name that seems perfect for a puppy may seem undignified when that puppy reaches adulthood.

Avoid sound-alike names. Names that sound like either common commands or the names of other people in your house will quickly confuse your dog. For example, the name *Noah* wouldn't work, because it sounds too much like the word *no*. Similarly, if your daughter's name is Jenny, you probably want to avoid naming your dog Penny.

Don't choose a name associated with negative behavior. Prime examples here: aggressive names for dogs.

Pick a name you can use in public. Naming a dachshund Boner may seem funny at first, but could backfire if you have to call your wiener dog in a crowded public place—especially if there are children around!

If you're stumped, go on-line. The World Wide Web has lots of sites that not only list common dog names but also have searchable databases that can help you match your dog's breed and personality to potential monikers. Type "common dog names" into any search engine, and you'll come up with scores of sites that are chock-full of ideas.

Follow the leaders. If you can't come up with something suitable on your own, consider what's worked for other people and pooches. For example, the New York City Health Department, which is responsible for doling out dog licenses, reports that the most popular names for Big Apple dogs in 2000 were Max, Lucky, Rocky, Princess, Lady, Buddy, Shadow, Coco, Brandy, and Sandy.

CHAPTER 7

Dealing with Your New Dog's Health Issues

DID YOU THINK you could relax once you brought your new dog home? Not quite yet.

One of the first things you need to do after bringing home your new canine companion is to take him for his first visit to the veterinarian you've selected. You don't need to make this visit immediately after your dog crosses your threshold, but you should plan on doing it very soon thereafter—certainly no longer than forty-eight hours or so.

This first tête-à-tête between your pooch and your vet is important for several reasons. First, it gives you and your dog a chance to get better acquainted with a person who will play a key role in safeguarding your dog's health. In addition, the exam that occurs during this visit will allow your veterinarian to get acquainted with your dog's inner workings—and to provide a basis for comparison during subsequent exams. And finally, the exam may uncover unknown or hidden health problems besetting your new canine companion, enabling you and your vet to begin solving those problems right away.

Your dog and your vet should get acquainted soon after the dog comes home.

To speed up the getting-to-know-you process, you should bring whatever health records you've been given for your new dog and, if possible, a sample of the dog's poop. The records will help the vet determine what shots and other medications your dog will need. The stool sample will be examined for the presence of parasites, such as worms.

In addition to examining your dog's health records and analyzing the stool sample, the vet probably also will:

- Weigh your dog
- Take his temperature
- Measure his pulse and respiration
- Check his body for lumps, bumps, rashes, parasites, and signs of infection
- Look inside his ears for signs of parasites and infection
- Peer into his eyes for signs of any abnormalities
- Check the genitals—in males, to see whether both testicles are fully descended; in females to make sure there's no discharge from the vagina

- Check the rest of the dog's body for rashes, parasites, and signs of infection
- Check the gums and teeth for overall health and proper tooth formation

After the vet examines your dog, she may give him one or more immunizations, depending on your four-legged friend's age and health status. Those shots might include:

- A single shot to prevent rabies, a disease that's deadly to both dogs and people. Today, wild animals such as raccoons, bats, skunks, and foxes are much more likely than dogs to have this disease—but a bite from an infected critter can pass the disease on to your dog, who in turn can transmit it to you. And once symptoms become apparent in either the human or canine victim, the disease is fatal. That's why the law just about everywhere requires that domestic animals be vaccinated against rabies. Puppies usually get their first rabies shots at around sixteen weeks of age and a booster about a year after that. Adult dogs get their rabies shots every one to three years, depending on local laws.
- A combination shot to guard against other serious diseases, such as parvovirus, distemper, hepatitis, leptospirosis, and parainfluenza. Depending on your dog's health and your veterinarian's philosophy regarding immunizations, your dog may be given this combo shot, often called the DHLPP, every one to three years. Puppies are generally given four of these shots spread out over three-week intervals. The first shot is usually administered when a puppy is about six weeks old.
- A shot to prevent bordatella, or kennel cough, if you plan to board your dog frequently, or take him to places where other dogs gather, such as a dog park.

Depending on what your vet sees in the stool sample, she might also give your dog medication to rid him of any parasites that are

SAYING NO TO FLEAS
(AND OTHER FREELOADERS)

Cartoons of yore often depicted mangy-looking dogs who were con-
stantly scratching themselves, presumably because they were being bitten by fleas. Such depictions often were designed to elicit laughter
among the humans who viewed the cartoon. But in real life, fleas are
no laughing matter—for your dog or for you.

Fleas can make your dog's life miserable. Their bites can cause any
dog to get itchy—but if your particular canine companion is allergic to
those flea bites, he's likely to scratch himself so much that he'll lose part
of his coat, cause his skin to bleed, and open the door to all kinds of
tough-to-treat infections. And even if he's not allergic, a dog who gets
no relief from fleas may become anemic, due to the fleas' preference for
dining on canine blood. Moreover, fleas are equal opportunity parasites;
they're more than capable of infesting you and the other human members of your family. When they do, you'll be scratching just as much as
your dog does.

Fortunately, the twenty-first-century dog and his people can get
permanent relief from fleas. In recent years, pharmaceutical companies
have unveiled a variety of products that successfully eradicate fleas.
Some do their jobs by stopping the flea's eggs from developing, thus
causing the population to die off because it can't reproduce. Others kill
the adult fleas that make the mistake of biting the treated dog.

Even better is the fact that many flea-control products are masters
of multitasking. The same product that stops flea eggs from developing
also kills parasites such as heartworm (which is often fatal if untreated),
hookworm, roundworm, and whipworm. A product that zaps adult
fleas does the same to ticks, which can carry Lyme disease and other
dangerous maladies. Both are available only with a veterinarian's
prescription.

Although some flea control products are available over the counter,
it's far better to let your vet prescribe products that you can count on to
get rid of these annoying pests—permanently.

hitching a ride with him. These unwelcome freeloaders include roundworms (which are very common in puppies), hookworms, and whipworms. It's important to evict any of these critters, because they can deplete your dog's energy and health, especially if he is a puppy. The vet might also suggest that you administer meds to combat other parasites such as fleas and heartworms.

Although antiworming products are available over the counter, it's better to steer clear of these products and rely on the remedies that your vet prescribes. That's because the meds your vet orders will be designed to deal specifically with those critters that are besieging your canine companion.

And, if necessary, your vet will talk to you about arranging to have your puppy or dog spayed or neutered. Your contract with the animal shelter, rescue group, or breeder probably requires you to have this procedure performed on your four-legged friend. For puppies, the procedure generally takes place at around six months of age, although some veterinarians do it earlier. Adult dogs can get fixed at just about any time, except when a female is already in heat (a period of about three weeks when she has a bloody discharge from her vagina and is receptive to mating with a male dog).

SAYING NO TO SHOTS

Some people have told me that I shouldn't give my dog a bunch of shots every year. They say that yearly immunizations actually can make a dog sick. What's the story here?

The common practice of giving yearly immunizations to a dog has become quite controversial among veterinarians and their clients. Some veterinarians now question whether a dog needs yearly shots in order to be protected against disease and point out that human beings don't need or get annual immunizations. In addition, research is beginning to indicate that vaccines for dogs are effective for longer periods of time than previously thought.

Others believe that giving the annual shots can actually send a dog's immune system into overdrive, triggering the onset of one or more autoimmune diseases. An autoimmune disease is a condition in which the immune system attacks the body of the affected individual, rather than the disease. For example, a condition called symmetrical lupoid onychodystrophy (yes, that is a mouthful!) is believed to be an autoimmune disease that causes the dog's immune system to attack the animal's nails, causing the nails to break, crumble, and/or fall off. A more serious autoimmune disease is lupus, a condition in which the autoimmune system attacks and rejects multiple systems of the body (People can get lupus, too.).

Unfortunately, there's no method that precisely measures whether a vaccine in an individual dog is still working. Veterinarians can try to measure the level of effectiveness by performing a test called a titer, but such tests are not always accurate.

These considerations put the conscientious dog owner in a real pickle. On the one hand, the owner wants to make sure that her canine companion is fully protected against diseases such as distemper and parvovirus. Both diseases can prove fatal to a dog, especially if the animal is a puppy. On the other hand, the owner certainly doesn't want to undertake a regimen that could prove harmful to the dog over the long term.

Some veterinarians have come up with compromises that call for continued immunizations—but not every year. For example, the faculty of Colorado State University's veterinary school recommends that puppies continue to receive the usual full complement of shots and that boosters be given upon reaching adulthood. After that, though, Colorado State recommends that shots be given every three years instead of annually.

The big exception to any debate about shots is the immunization given for rabies. State laws require that dogs and cats be immunized against this always-lethal disease—not only for their protection, but also to protect the people who can contract the disease from them. Some states require annual rabies shots; others mandate shots every three years.

You and your veterinarian need to determine what your particular dog's immunization schedule should be. But whether you opt for annual shots or immunizations every three years, it's important to take your canine companion to your vet for a physical every year, without fail.

EARLY SPAYING OR NEUTERING

My vet wants me to spay my puppy now, when she's only nine weeks old! I thought female dogs shouldn't be spayed until after they went into heat for the first time. What's going on?

Clearly you have never lived with, ahem, a true bitch in heat. Those who have can tell you that it is a messy, multiweek affair, characterized by drippy, bloody stains. They can also relate horror stories having to fight off male dogs who seem to materialize out of nowhere at the prospect of finding a little canine romance. (This is assuming, of course, that you don't want your female dog to have puppies.)

But even if living through a dog's heat season weren't such a hassle, veterinarians have agreed for quite a while that there's no reason to wait till the first heat—which generally occurs at seven to nine months of age—to spay a female dog. More recently, though, some veterinarians and humane organizations have advocated very early spaying and neutering.

The humane groups are rightly concerned about holding down pet population growth. Veterinarians point out that the earlier a dog is spayed or neutered, the less risk there will be that the animal will develop certain cancers or infections. The vets have found that a seven-to-nine-week-old puppy heals much more quickly from the spay/neuter procedure than is the case with an animal who's even a few months older. Moreover, today's veterinarians know how to safely anesthetize very young canine patients, which means that the procedure is now just as safe for them as it is for slightly older dogs.

If your vet recommends early spaying for your nine-week-old female dog (or neutering for a similarly aged male), I'd go ahead. Make sure, however, that your vet first draws a little blood from your puppy and sends it to a laboratory for analysis. The blood work will help ensure that your puppy can tolerate the anesthesia that he'll need for the procedure. In fact, it's a good idea for any dog of any age to have a blood analysis (what vets call a "blood panel") done *prior* to any surgical procedure.

SIGNS OF DOGGIE SICKNESS

I know that a cold, wet nose doesn't necessarily mean that my dog isn't sick. But how can I tell when my dog is sick—short of taking her temperature?

Healthy puppies and dogs show it: Their eyes are clear and bright, without any goop leaking from them; their ears are clean and odor-free; their doggie breath is not overwhelming; their noses are moist but not runny; and their coats shine. There are no bald patches on their coats; their skin is clear and snaps back when pulled (if it doesn't, the dog is dehydrated). Healthy dogs move easily, without limping, and are interested in the world around them. They enjoy eating good grub and drinking fresh water. And because what goes in must also come out, healthy dogs poop and pee regularly, too.

The absence of any of the above hallmarks of good canine health should alert you to a possible problem. Such problems don't necessarily constitute emergencies, but they do require your attention—and, possibly, a call to your vet if things don't improve within a day or two. (For unmistakable signs of emergencies, see the "When to See the Vet Right Away" box in this chapter.)

As for taking your dog's temperature, you can do it much the same way it used to be done for a human infant. Get a pet thermometer, or a rectal thermometer that you use solely for your dog. Lubricate the end with a little bit of petroleum jelly, and then place the thermometer in the dog's rectum. Hold your dog still and leave the thermometer in for about sixty seconds. Then, check the reading.

A dog's normal temperature falls between 99 and 102.5 degrees Fahrenheit. If your dog's temperature varies significantly from that range—and especially if she's showing other signs of illness—put in a call to your vet. On the other hand, if she's been running around, is excited or nervous, and shows a temperature above 102.5 degrees, you don't need to worry—as long as she shows no other signs of being sick. My own dog consistently exhibits a temperature of 103 to 103.5 degrees whenever he visits our vet. Generally, though, he's been pacing and panting nervously for several minutes before his temp gets taken, so his doctor doesn't find the high reading to be any cause for concern.

GETTING STOOL SAMPLES

How can I get a stool sample from my new dog without getting the stool on me?

Getting a stool sample is simply a matter of bagging it. Find an oblong plastic bag, such as a bread bag or the bag your newspaper arrives in. When your pooch makes a deposit, place your hand inside the fully extended bag, so that the bag comes over your hand like a glove. Pick up the poop with your bagged hand; then, grasp the open end of the bag with your other hand, and pull it inside out. Now the poop will be inside the bag—and neither of your hands will have touched the offending material. Knot the bag and place it in an airtight container (a clean, empty yogurt or margarine container that has an airtight lid works great).

Incidentally, a stool sample should be no more than twelve hours old. An older sample may not yield accurate results.

GETTING A URINE SAMPLE

What do I do if my vet wants a urine sample? How can I get a sample without getting some of my dog's pee on me?

Here again, an oblong plastic bag such as a newspaper bag or bread bag does the trick. Before you take your dog for the potty break during which you'll collect the sample, get an oblong plastic bag and an airtight plastic container with a lid. A clean, empty margarine container or yogurt container with a matching lid each work well.

While you walk your canine companion, watch for signs that he's about to take a leak. Such signs include intense sniffing, circling, and pacing. Quickly place the bag over your hand like a glove, and hold the open container with your bagged hand. As your dog begins to urinate, push the container under your dog's urethra or penis. Let a little bit of urine accumulate in the container (you don't need more than about a tablespoonful), then remove the container and put the lid on it. Bring the sample to your vet as soon as possible.

GIVING YOUR POOCH A PILL

I'm supposed to give my dog a pill to keep him from getting fleas and ticks, but she won't take it. What should I do?

Dogs generally do not take pills voluntarily. To ensure that they get their meds, their human guardians need to either fool them into ingesting the pills or give the pills to them directly.

The first approach is probably preferable for person and pooch alike. This tactic simply involves hiding the pill in a dog's favorite regular food (canned food makes a better hiding place than dry food does). The dog will eat everything in his dish, including the well-hidden pill, and be none the wiser.

A variation on this approach is to find a special, soft treat that your dog adores, and hide the pill in that. Two such treats that are practically guaranteed to get the job done are cream cheese and peanut butter.

If, however, your clever canine discovers your trickery—either by spitting the pill out or eating around it—you'll have to be more direct. In that case, here's what to do:

- Gently place your thumb and forefinger at the midpoints of either side of your dog's upper lip. He will automatically open his mouth.
- With your other hand, place the pill at the very base of your dog's tongue.
- Hold your dog's mouth closed, with his nose pointed upward.
- Rub your dog's throat gently. You should see her swallow the pill.
- Wash your hands! (They'll be coated with canine saliva)

If neither approach works, consult your vet to see if there's some other way to give your dog her medicine.

FLUNKING A PHYSICAL

We took our new puppy to the veterinarian for his first physical, and he didn't exactly get a clean bill of health. Not only did he have worms, but the vet also found a skin infection and a possible heart murmur. We're wondering whether we should keep this dog, or whether to return him to the breeder and find a dog who's really healthy.

It's incredibly painful to discover that your pooch isn't perfect after all. However, two of the problems you describe—the worms and the skin infection—may not be a big deal. Almost every puppy gets round-worms, and a couple of rounds of deworming meds from your vet will eliminate them. Many puppies also develop a skin infection that's known as "puppy pyoderma," which is easily cleared up with a short course of antibiotics.

The heart murmur, however, may be another matter. You need to have a heart-to-heart (pun not intended!) talk with your veterinarian about your puppy's particular heart problem: the causes, the treatment options, the costs of such treatment, and the prognosis. Only then can you make a reasoned, educated decision about whether to keep this particular pup.

This situation exemplifies why any contract from a breeder should contain provisions allowing you to return a puppy and to choose a new one if the initial health check reveals problems that you're not prepared to deal with.

THE ALL-KNOWING VET

How can my vet know how to treat something like, say, heart disease in an older dog, but also know how to care for a puppy? Can I really count on just one person to give my dog the care he needs from puppyhood to old age?

The answer to your question is, "Probably not." No single veterinarian can cover all the bases involved in twenty-first-century veterinary medicine. With treatment for dogs and other companion animals becoming as sophisticated as it is for people, expecting one vet to do it all would be like asking a pediatrician to suddenly become an oncologist or a cardiac surgeon. It's just not possible.

The veterinary profession recognizes this impossibility. That's why, as the technology for treating our canine companions has grown, the veterinary profession has developed a plethora of specialties. In all probability, your dog will visit at least a few of them. For example, in his six years of life, my own dog, Cory, has visited a veterinary dermatologist and a veterinary ophthalmologist for specialized treatment of various ailments he's had.

The American Veterinary Medical Association, which is the national professional organization for vets who work in the United States, lists twenty veterinary specialty organizations on its website, www.avma.org. Some of those organizations, such as the American College of Poultry Veterinarians, aren't likely to include vets who would treat your four-legged friend. But there are plenty of others, such as the American Veterinary Dental College, the American College of Veterinary Dermatology, and the American College of Veterinary Ophthalmology. Other specialty groups deal with anesthesiology, cardiology, behavior, emergency care, internal medicine, radiology, surgery, toxicology, and oncology.

The members of each of these specialty groups are veterinarians who have completed postgraduate work in their respective subjects. Then, they must pass rigorous examinations designed to test their knowledge in their specialties. If they do pass, their specialty organization certifies them as being qualified specialists in their particular fields of veterinary medicine. When you hear that a veterinary specialist is "board-certified," you can be sure that the specialist brings a boatload of credentials to the work that he or she does with animal patients.

Veterinary specialists sometimes cluster around large practices—for example, near Washington, D.C., the Southpaws Veterinary Referral Center includes specialists in animal behavior, emergency care, holistic medicine, internal medicine, neurology, oncology, radiology, surgery, orthopedics, and holistic medicine. In less-populated areas, veterinary specialists can be found at universities or colleges that have schools of veterinary medicine. Either way, if your dog ever needs specialized care that your regular vet can't provide, she'll refer you to the appropriate specialist—just as your own doctor does for you.

WHEN TO SEE THE VET RIGHT AWAY

Most of the health problems your puppy or dog will face don't need to be treated right away. They merely require calling your vet and booking a same-day or next-day appointment (or a visit on some other day, if that's what your vet suggests). However, some symptoms and events demand immediate attention no matter when they occur—even on the weekend or other time that your vet's office normally is closed. Here's a list of some of those symptoms and circumstances:

1 **Clear signs of pain.** These include panting while resting; rapid, loud, or otherwise labored breathing; inability to relax; and/or lost appetite. The pain could result from a multitude of illnesses or injuries that only your vet is qualified to diagnose.

2 **Gums that are pale pink, white, or bluish in color.** The normal color of a dog's gums is a bright, robust pink. Pale pink, white, or bluish gums are a sign of shock or internal bleeding—both of which demand immediate attention.

3 **Extreme tiredness.** A normally perky pooch who seems unusually tired for more than a day or two could have a major health problem. Again, though, the problem is something that only a vet can diagnose—so get your dog to one immediately.

4 **Swollen stomach.** A swelled up abdomen, particularly when coupled with restlessness and labored breathing, are symptoms of bloat, a condition that is fatal if left untreated. The condition mainly affects large and extra-large dogs. A study at Purdue University identified the following breeds as having the greatest risk of bloat: Akita, bloodhound, collie, Great Dane, Irish setter, Irish wolfhound, Newfoundland, Rottweiler, Saint Bernard, standard poodle, and Weimaraner.

5 **A clearly traumatic event.** Examples include such things as being hit by a car, a near-drowning, a fall from a significant height, being in a car accident, an animal bite, or suffering from excessive heat (heat exhaustion) or cold (hypothermia). Even if the dog appears to be okay, take him to a vet right away.

6 Ingesting a forbidden substance. If you even suspect that your dog has ingested a poisonous plant or household item, or something else that doesn't belong in his system (e.g., socks), get him to your vet immediately, so that you can forestall life-threatening problems.

7 Excessive vomiting and diarrhea. A puppy who's upchucking or defecating more than once an hour, or an adult dog who's doing the same every half-hour, needs immediate attention. That's because too much vomiting and diarrhea can dehydrate the dog or bring the animal's blood sugar dangerously low.

8 Collapse, seizure, or fainting. Pooches who suddenly lose their footing could be suffering from any one of a number of serious maladies, all of which need veterinary treatment.

9 Straining to pee. A dog who tries to piddle, only to have little or nothing come out, may be experiencing kidney problems or a urinary blockage. See your vet immediately.

10 Change in one or both eyes. Sudden blindness, sudden redness, or other abrupt changes in the look or condition of a dog's eye can indicate that the dog has glaucoma or another serious eye condition. Such problems need to be treated promptly.

11 Your intuition. If you just have the feeling that there is something very wrong with your canine companion—if he's acting or appears very different from what you believe to be normal—bring him to your vet, or at least put in a call. Most vets have found that an owner can sometimes sense a potential problem with her pet before the tools of the veterinary trade can.

If your dog faces a medical emergency when your vet's office isn't open, don't despair. Many veterinary practices provide clients with an after-hours telephone number to call. In addition, many urban areas have clinics that are open only during the night and on weekends. Before it's necessary, check with your own vet to see what his after-hours policies are, and whether an emergency veterinary service is available in your area.

CHAPTER **8**

Dealing with Your New Dog's Emotional Issues

DEALING WITH YOUR new dog's health issues is just one part of helping him adjust to life with you. That's because dogs also have emotional issues—and those issues are likely to be front and center when you first welcome him into your family.

Not so long ago, any scientist worth his salt would have taken issue with the very thought that dogs have emotions, much less issues. I can't tell you how many interviews I've conducted with animal behavior experts in which the expert chides me for assuming that animals have feelings like we humans do and warns me not to anthropomorphize. Anthropomorphizing, in case you haven't been accused of it, is the act of attributing human motives and emotions to an animal's behavior. For many scientists, guarding against such attributions has extended to questioning whether animals even feel emotions, much less whether those emotions are similar to those felt by human beings.

In recent years, though, some experts have begun to rethink their stances on anthropomorphizing—and, by extension, on animal emotions. And in doing so, they're probably acknowledging what people who live with dogs already know: Our canine companions (and other animals) *do* have feelings.

These researchers have taken the time to painstakingly observe the behavior of not only dogs but also cats, livestock, and wild animals. Led by forward-thinking scientists such as Marc Bekoff, a biology professor at the University of Colorado, experts are beginning to pool their observations of animal behavior in an effort to better understand the world we share with our fellow creatures. And they're

Dogs' emotions are easy to read—if you understand canine body language.

becoming increasingly willing to accept the idea that dogs and other nonhuman beings have rich emotional lives. Acceptance of that idea, however, does not mean that we always understand what those emotions are, much less how nonhuman animals express them.

For example, many people believe that a dog wags his tail only when he feels happy—but animal behaviorists know better. A dog who's holding his tail up high and wagging it stiffly is more likely to be defending his turf, or otherwise be on the brink of being aggressive. A dog who holds his wagging tail very low may be frightened or apprehensive, rather than happy. (For more information on canine body language, check out the box "What Your Dog Is Trying to Tell You" later in this chapter.)

Still, the effort to understand what a dog is feeling when he joins a new household can go a long way toward helping that dog make a smooth adjustment to that household—and can accelerate the development of a lifelong bond between that dog and his new people.

If your new dog is a puppy, the issues are likely to be fairly straightforward, simply because he doesn't have much of a past. Before meeting you, all he probably ever knew was life with his mother and siblings. All were probably cared for mainly by one person, the breeder, with perhaps a little assistance from other members of the breeder's family. Consequently, a puppy's emotional issues are likely to be centered around dealing with his sudden (and, to him, inexplicable) separation from the dogs and people that he's been with for all of his young life. Many such puppies show their distress over this separation by whining, yelping, and otherwise carrying on at night, when they miss the comfort of their littermates the most. During the day, such puppies may tire easily, and act bewildered at all the new sights, sounds, and people they're encountering.

Other than being overwhelmed by all the changes suddenly cascading through their lives, puppies are dealing with issues that relate more to inexperience than to emotions. They need help trying to make sense of a world that, to them, has been turned upside down, and to find ways to feel comfortable with change. Chapter twelve, "Socializing Your New Dog," tackles the process of helping your canine baby cope smoothly with at least most of what life is going to hand him. This process, which experts call socialization, is crucial to helping your puppy grow into a happy, well-adjusted adult dog.

Some adult dogs, alas, haven't had such happy puppyhoods. These dogs may not have had the tender loving care that a conscientious human guardian provides. Some have experienced neglect or even abuse. All have had to deal with loss. In short, every adult dog has a past, and many carry some emotional baggage. If you're adopting such a dog, you need to help ease that burden.

For example, a dog who's grieving over the loss of a previous human companion may not want to eat or may be timid about interacting with her new family members. A dog whose past includes having been hit with long-handled objects may cringe if she sees a cane or an umbrella. Other adult dogs may freak out at the sound of thunder or the sight of lightning; still others can't bear to be left alone. And still others may have prejudices against certain ethnic groups or a particular gender—prejudices that have a peculiar way of turning up at the most embarrassing times.

As you'll see in the questions and answers that follow, there are several tried-and-true ways to help dogs deal with their emotional issues. Many involve a process called desensitization: helping a dog to become less sensitive to whatever particular issue is bothering him. Desensitization involves exposing a dog very slowly to whatever triggers his fear or otherwise negative reaction. As his tolerance for the trigger increases, the length of time you expose him to that trigger also increases. Eventually, whatever initially bothered him may not faze him at all.

Another technique involves figuring out what's behind your dog's reaction. An animal whose hackles rise when she's around members of a particular ethnic group might have endured some rough treatment at the hands of someone from that group. Here, your task is to help your dog learn that one person's bad behavior doesn't mean that an entire group of people will be guilty of the same. You'll help your canine companion learn to associate the objects of her prejudice with enjoyable activities, not unhappy memories.

Here, then, are a few examples of canine emotional issues, how to help your new dog deal with them, and what to do when your dog's problem seems to be beyond your ability to solve.

HOUSETRAINED DOG PEES INDOORS

The shelter told me my new, two-year-old Lab-shepherd mix is housetrained—but in the week she's been with me, she's made a puddle at my feet almost every time I've walked into my house. Did the shelter just tell me she was housetrained so that I'd adopt her? Have I been duped?

Probably not. Your new canine companion may very well have impeccable bathroom manners. Her behavior when you arrive home has nothing to do with potty protocol. Instead, she's showing you respect, canine-style.

That's because for dogs, the act of urinating is much more than the emptying of one's bladder—it's also a way of communicating. Chapter fourteen, "Housetraining Your New Dog," will discuss pooches' potty talk in detail. For now, though, you only need to understand that a dog who pees when you arrive home is basically saying, "Welcome home, O lord and master."

Of course, neither you nor your floor benefits from such displays of canine reverence. To forestall those displays, you need to come across a little less like a lord and master and more like someone whom your deferential doggie can relax with.

Begin by ignoring your dog when you arrive home. That's right: Simply walk in your door and walk past her. Above all, don't look at her. Dogs interpret a direct look from another dog—or from a person—as a statement of dominance. Consequently, when you look at your about-to-piddle pooch, she thinks you're saying, "I am the king of this domicile." She then urinates to tell you that she's happy to be your loyal subject.

Once you're in the door and have walked past her, sit on the floor —and continue to refrain from looking at her. Peering down at your dog from your standing height simply reinforces the statement of dominance that a direct stare seems to make. By sitting on the floor, you're getting down to your dog's level and helping her to feel more relaxed.

Stay on the floor until she calms down. When she does, she's likely to come over and sniff you. When that happens, pet her very gently and talk with her softly. Only when you feel sure that she's collected herself should you try to look at her.

PEEING INDOORS, TAKE TWO

My nine-month-old Rottweiler is housetrained except for one thing: He's using my living room sofa for pee-pee target practice! How do I get him to stop doing this?

Your Rottweiler's behavior is another example of canine toilet talk—although, unlike the very respectful dog featured in the previous question, your pooch's message probably has nothing to do with being intimidated or feeling deferential. Instead, your Rottie may have turf issues. In other words, he may be anointing your sofa because he wants to tell the world that he considers the sofa to be his. Experts call this behavior "marking."

Dogs feel the need to map out their territory for several reasons. One reason is to demonstrate to an interloper—human or canine—that he, Fido, owns the spot being anointed. Another reason is to simply announce to the world that they have passed by a particular spot. This is what many male dogs are doing when they give in to their compulsions to lift their legs and christen every vertical surface they pass while being walked.

To rid your Rottie of his compulsion to leave his mark on your sofa—or anywhere else—here's what to do:

Neuter now. Most dogs who feel compelled to mark are un-neutered males who want to demonstrate their canine machismo.

Removing the impetus to express that machismo could very well end the marking behavior completely.

Clean up completely. As you'll see in chapter fourteen, failure to clean up an unauthorized whiz will almost certainly prompt the dog to do an encore on the very same spot. Use a commercial pet stain cleaner to get rid of not only the puddle but also that come-hither odor.

Catch him. If you see your canine guy start to lift his leg in a forbidden spot, startle him with either a loud voice or by clapping your hands. The suddenness of the noise may be enough to interrupt him before he opens his floodgates. Then, get him to his outdoor potty spot as quickly as possible.

Reassure him. If your dog's marking behavior is in response to the arrival of a human household guest, have the guest play with the dog and otherwise reassure him that there's nothing for the dog to worry about.

Give him a refresher course. Until you get the marking behavior under control, you need to give your canine companion a remedial course in housetraining. See chapter fourteen.

COPING WITH A DESTRUCTO DOG

When I left my new dog home alone for a couple of hours, I came back to find my living room looking totally trashed. My dog had chewed open a seat cushion, scattered the cushion stuffing all over the place, knocked over a lamp, and chewed a crater into the middle of a throw rug. I can't afford to replace my furniture and carpet every time I go out. What can I do?

Destructiveness is a common result of a dog's reaction to anxiety over being left alone. It's a fairly frequent problem among dogs, particularly those who have lost one home and are getting used to another one. Experts call this problem "separation anxiety"—and solving it calls for a multipronged approach. Here are some ideas:

Get her moving. A tired dog is less likely to go on a loneliness-induced rampage when you're gone—simply because she'll be too fatigued to feel lonely or anxious about spending some solo time. Before you head out the door, take her for a long walk or jog, or find another way to get her the exercise she needs.

Feed her twice a day. All dogs generally do better with two meals a day than with one, but the twice-daily regimen works especially well with dogs who have separation anxiety. That's because a dog's anxiety may increase when she's hungry.

Put on the radio. Many dogs feel soothed if there's music playing softly during the day. Choose carefully, though: Some low-key classical or New Age music is more likely to do the trick than something from the local alternative rock station.

Downplay your comings and goings. As much as you hate to part from your canine companion—and as glad as you are to see her when you come home—keep the hellos and good-byes low-key for her sake. If you don't make a big deal of your absences, she'll learn not to make a big deal of them either.

Vary your routine. A varied routine makes it tougher for your dog to figure out that you're leaving—and if he doesn't know that you're leaving, he won't be as anxious. If your dog knows, for example, that when you pick up the keys you're about to leave the house, try varying your predeparture routine. Pick up your keys —but then stay in the house. Put on your shoes—but then take them off and stay home. Put on your lipstick right before you leave instead of a few minutes before.

Get him some company. If you need to be away all day on a regular basis (and most of us do), consider enrolling your dog in a doggie day care center, or find someone who can exercise him during the middle of the day. The company may be all he needs to take his mind off your absence.

Confine him. Your dog won't be able to damage your living room if he doesn't have access to it. Find a room in your house that is more impervious to the ravages of canine anxiety—a laundry room or kitchen are both ideal—and place your dog there. Put his crate there, too, as well as some water and other gear. However, do not put him in his crate: It's cruel to keep a dog in his crate for more than a couple of hours at a time.

Give him a job. If your dog has a task to perform while you're gone, he'll forget to be anxious about your absence. Many experts suggest filling a toy such as a Kong or a Busta cube with tasty treats and giving the toy to your dog just before you leave. He'll become so engrossed in ferreting out the treats that he'll forget to miss you.

See an expert. If all else fails, take your dog to your veterinarian for evaluation. Either he or a veterinary behaviorist can help you come up with other ideas for easing your canine companion's apprehensions. One possible option is a prescription for an antianxiety medication, such as Clomicalm, which is approved specifically for easing canine separation anxiety. Meds aren't cure-alls for this problem, but when used in combination with other steps taken to modify the dog's behavior, they can be surprisingly helpful.

THE PREJUDICED POOCH

My newly adopted dog—I got her from a shelter—doesn't like men. She growls and slinks around whenever a man gets too close. I'm worried that her behavior could derail any future romances I might have.

Before you worry about your long-term romantic prospects, it might be a good idea to put yourself in your dog's place. From her point of view, she may have very good reasons for being a bit of a sexist.

The shelter may be able to tell you what your dog's previous background was. Did she live in a home where she was abused, neglected, or otherwise mistreated by a man? Did she live in a household where there were no men at all? Those are just two possible reasons why your dog doesn't think very highly of y-chromosomed humans.

Once you develop a bit of empathy for your canine companion, you'll be in a better position to ask your male friends—romantic and otherwise—to help her overcome her antimale bias. Don't force your dog and the guys in your life to spend a lot of time together, at least not right away. Instead, create brief encounters between them—but make sure those encounters are pleasant for the dog. The objective here is to help the dog associate the pleasurable experiences with the presence of your male friends.

For example, have your new boyfriend give your dog her favorite treat whenever he comes to pick you up. He need not even give it directly to the dog: Just leaving it on the floor in her presence is a good start. Eventually, though, your dog is likely to be willing to take the treat out of your boyfriend's hand. That particular development probably will happen faster if your boyfriend is the only person to give your dog this particular treat.

Once your dog begins to rely on your boyfriend to supply her with these special goodies, she will have taken the first big step in associating him with something enjoyable. At that point, he can try sitting on the floor and allowing your dog to come over and sniff him. When she's giving him those friendly once-overs on a regular basis, he might try gently patting her on the side of her body (not her head, which could startle her and make her skittish). Once he's able to do that, you can consider the battle won.

Incidentally, similar tactics work on dogs with other prejudices. The idea is to associate the object of such prejudice with something pleasant, rather than unpleasant.

RIDING IN CARS WITH CANINES

The very thought of riding in a car seems to give my new dog the willies. He shakes like a leaf and drools whenever he's an auto passenger. I want to be able to take him places with me; will he ever get used to being in a car?

There's a good chance that your dog can learn to love riding in your car—if you give him time to get used to the idea and if you can show him that riding in the car does not automatically lead to something unpleasant.

Too many dogs get car rides only when they have to visit their veterinarians. While we humans realize that our vets are key players in the effort to maintain the good health of our dogs, our canine companions may not share this realization. To them, a visit to the vet may mean that something not so fun is going to happen: at the very least, a round of being poked at, and getting stuck with a needle. The dog whose only auto excursions lead to the vet's office will, understandably, equate the car with the dreaded destination.

For that reason alone, it's a good idea to accustom your dog to what, for him, may be a revolutionary concept: Riding in a car can be fun. If possible, start simply by sitting in the car with him for a few minutes. Pet him and tell him what a brave boy he is. Then, take him out of the car and give him a treat. Keep doing this until the two of you can sit in the car for about ten minutes without him freaking out.

Once you've achieved that milestone, you're ready for the next step: a short drive. Put your dog in the car and drive next door with him. That's right, just next door. At that point, stop the car, praise your pooch, and give him a treat. Continue with this procedure until you're riding around the block with aplomb. At that point, it's probably fair to say that your canine can cope with a car ride.

Of course, during any auto ride, make sure your dog is as securely fastened in his seat as you are in yours. Make sure you use his doggie seat belt or—if he's small enough—put him in his crate and secure the crate in the car with a seat belt.

THE VACUUM-HATING DOG

My new dog is very hostile to my vacuum cleaner. Whenever I vacuum my carpets, he snarls and charges at the machine. How can I break him of this habit?

To end your pooch's vacuum-attacking ways, you need to desensitize him to the presence of the machine. Begin by simply bringing the vacuum cleaner out into the middle of the room and leaving it there; do not turn it on. Let your dog approach the machine and sniff it. When he does, tell him what a good, brave boy he is, and give him a treat. (For information on good treats to give your dog, check out chapter nine.)

Once your dog is approaching the vacuum cleaner with equanimity, try turning it on—but only for a couple of seconds. Then turn it off and encourage your dog to check out the machine. Praise him lavishly when he does, and give him a treat. Continue this process until you're able to keep the vacuum on for two or three minutes.

Now you're ready to start moving the vacuum around while it's turned on. Turn on the machine and move it around for a minute or two. Then turn it off and encourage your dog to sniff the machine. Praise him and give him a treat when he does. Continue this routine until you're able to finally vacuum your carpets without fear of any canine assaults.

If you think this sounds like a protracted process, you're absolutely right. It's perfectly understandable that you would conclude that breaking your canine companion of his vacuum-attacking habit is more trouble than it's worth. In that case, there's another, far quicker solution: Put your dog in his crate before you start vacuuming. You'll probably find—as I have with my vacuum-hating dog—that your pooch will feel relieved that he can't do his self-proclaimed duty to assault the big, bad sucking machine. He may even go to sleep in his crate, which will allow you to hunt down dust bunnies in relative peace.

CALLING IN A PRO

I've run out of ideas for dealing with my dog's behavioral problem— and a friend of mine said, only half-jokingly, that maybe my dog needs a shrink! Are there really psychologists for dogs? And if so, can they really help?

As far as I know there are no psychologists for dogs per se—but some people with degrees in psychology (and other subjects) do decide to provide similar services for dogs and cats. These individuals are called behaviorists. There are two types of accredited behaviorists: certified applied animal behaviorists, and veterinary behaviorists.

A veterinary behaviorist is a veterinarian who has successfully completed the process of board certification by the American College of Veterinary Behaviorists (ACVB). A candidate for ACVB certification must complete an extensive course of postgraduate training and work experience in the field of animal behavior, pass a credential review, and pass an examination given by the ACVB. The certification process generally takes about two years—and that's two years in addition to the several years of undergraduate school and veterinary school needed for a person to become the veterinary equivalent of a general practitioner. A board-certified veterinary behaviorist may place not only the initials DVM or VMD after her name, but also the title Dipl. ACVB (for diplomate, American College of Veterinary Behaviorists).

Unlike a veterinary behaviorist, a certified applied animal behaviorist need not be a vet. However, the latter nevertheless has extensive training—generally a doctorate—in a biological or behavioral science such as psychology or biology, plus five years of professional experience. A veterinarian who wants to become a certified applied animal behaviorist must complete a two-year residency program in animal behavior that is approved by a university. The certifications for this type of behaviorist are conferred by the Animal Behavior Society (ABS).

Many veterinary behaviorists are associated with large universities that have colleges of veterinary medicine; a few are one of several specialists that work in large veterinary practices. Certified applied animal behaviorists work at universities or have private practices.

Either type of behaviorist can evaluate your dog and suggest ways to solve his problem that you might not have thought of. In addition, a veterinary behaviorist (or a certified applied animal behaviorist who is also a veterinarian) can prescribe medication to ease your dog's condition if the situation warrants.

If you're interested in bringing your dog to a behaviorist, it's best to start with your own veterinarian. Let her evaluate your canine companion; there may be ways to address your dog's problem without having to consult a behaviorist. If, however, she agrees that further help is needed, she can find the behaviorists who are closest to where you live and provide you with a referral.

WHAT YOUR DOG IS TRYING TO TELL YOU

To human beings, dogs can behave in some very perplexing ways. With a little investigating, though, most people can decode their dogs' behavior. Here are some clues:

Taking a bow. A dog who places his front legs along the ground while sticking his bottom up in the air is a dog who's asking you, his beloved pack leader, to do something—probably to play. Such a dog may also display a wagging tail and have his mouth open in a kind of doggy grin.

Bellying up. The pooch who rolls over onto his back, displays his belly, and spreads his hind legs apart is telling you that he recognizes your superior status in the pack. He may underscore that message by dribbling a little urine.

Telling tails. As explained earlier in this chapter, a wagging tail doesn't always denote canine happiness. When a dog's tail is wagging stiffly and pointed straight upward, he's more likely to attack than to play.

Happy growls. Just as a dog's wagging tail doesn't always mean that he's happy, a dog's growl doesn't always mean that he's hostile. A dog who's enjoying playtime is likely to growl softly, with the sound coming from his throat. He may also wag his tail loosely and display a doggie smile. By contrast, a dog who's about to bite may warn his victim with a growl that seems to come deep from his belly, and he'll underscore that warning with a stiffly wagging tail and a direct stare.

Giving a lick. Canine kisses also may have multiple meanings. A slurp to the lips may signal your dog's recognition that you're in charge. But dogs also lick your lips—or other parts of your body—simply because they're attracted to your scent.

CHAPTER 9

Feeding Your New Dog

THE ADAGE "YOU are what you eat" is just as true for dogs as it is for people. You can't expect your healthy new dog to stay that way unless you feed her a good, balanced diet.

But just what is a good, balanced canine diet? For a long time, the answer seemed simple: a bag of generic dry dog food that you tossed into your supermarket shopping cart and ran through the checkout line without doing very much damage to your weekly food budget. Now, however, we know better. We know that bargain-priced dog food may not be a bargain at all—simply because it's relatively low on the nutrients that a dog needs to stay healthy. Consequently, the unknowing consumer may end up spending more money than if he hadn't tried to feed his dog on the cheap.

Just what is that good stuff? In a nutshell, dogs need many of the same nutrients that people do. Those nutrients include:

• Proteins, which allow your dog's body to transform food into energy. They come from several sources, including meats, vegeta-

The cheapest dog food could turn out to be more expensive than you expected.

bles, and grains. But while it's possible to obtain protein from several sources, some sources offer better protein than others do. For example, your dog can digest a meat protein more easily than she can digest a grain protein. Therefore, a diet that has more of the former than the latter is better for your four-legged friend than the reverse.

• Carbohydrates, which also provide energy for your dog, although in a different way than proteins do. Plants—mainly grains and soybeans—are nature's carbohydrate factories, because they use sunlight to manufacture carbs from carbon dioxide and water.

• Fats, which are crucial to keeping a dog's hair and skin healthy, ensuring healthy digestion, and stabilizing the temperature of the dog's body. Fats are found not only in foods but also in special dietary supplements for dogs.

• Vitamins and minerals, which help the dog's body to use all the other nutrients properly. They also help sustain a dog's immune system, keep the coat healthy, and prevent a variety of health and behavioral problems. Some vitamins are already present in food, but they can also be given as supplements.

Having these essential nutrients in your dog's diet helps to keep her in prime condition—if they're combined in ways that enable them to work together effectively. Unfortunately, there's no single nutrient-balancing formula that optimizes the health of every single dog. The proper levels of nutrients that your particular canine companion requires depend on her age, her activity level, and her overall health.

A properly selected commercial dog food goes a long way toward striking the right nutrient balance for your very special four-legged friend. That's because they come in a variety of formulas designed to address different dogs' individual needs. Here are some examples:

- Life cycle diets balance nutrients to address the ways a dog's needs change as she ages. For example, a dog food designed for puppies usually has more protein in it than a food for older dogs. That's because puppies need the extra protein in order to grow.
- Activity diets are tailored to the lifestyles of individual dogs. As an example, a Border collie who herds sheep needs more protein than a shih tzu whose main job is to snuggle up on her special person's lap.
- Condition diets are designed to meet the special nutritional needs of dogs who have certain health problems. A food that contains extra fatty acids, for example, would be a good choice for a dog whose skin tends to be dry and flaky. Some condition diets are available at pet supermarkets and specialty stores, but many need to be prescribed by a veterinarian.

Most commercial dog food diets—general, life cycle, activity, or condition—come in two forms. One is dry food, also known as kibble, which consists of baked, bite-sized pellets of grains and meats. Kibble offers at least two pluses: It's easy to fix (just pour some into your dog's dish and let her have at it), and it's the more economical choice. The big minus for kibble—at least where canines are concerned—is that many dogs find it boring, especially if the kibble is the only food they eat. Another pitfall is that kibble contains a relatively high percentage of grains, which can make it less digestible than other types of dog food.

The other common form of commercial fare is canned food. If your pooch's palate dictated your dog food decision, canned food would probably win hands down. Canned food smells good to your four-legged friend and tastes even better. In addition, it contains lots of water, which makes for easy digesting. However, that same high-water content also means that the same amount of canned product may deliver much less nutrition for your dog food dollar than the equivalent amount of kibble does.

There's nothing that says, however, that you need to choose between canned food and kibble. In fact, many people don't. They want to combine the nutritional goodies of the dry food with the palate pleasure that canned food delivers. And, in fact, that's exactly what they do: They serve a mixture of the two.

When it comes to serving your dog, though, there is a third option: fixing your dog's food yourself.

The home-prepared doggie dinner (or breakfast) carries at least a couple of advantages. It allows you to exert complete control over what you feed your dog. You can also tailor your dog's dietary fare to whatever pleases her particular palate.

But the do-it-yourself option does have some minuses. For one thing, it's time consuming. And while you might not mind taking the time to fix Fido's fare yourself when you're at home, you might not feel like doing it (much less be able to do it) while you and your dog are on the road.

Another problem is that it can be difficult to put together meals that both please your dog and meet her nutritional needs. As with canned and dry food, though, the home-versus-commercial food choice need not be an either-or proposition. There's nothing wrong with using commercial food as the foundation for your dog's meals and garnishing them with some tasty homemade fare, such as pieces of lean meat or a few bite-sized bits of fruits or vegetables. Some blandishments may be just what's needed to turn a picky canine eater into an enthusiastic one.

If you're going to take over the preparation of your canine's cuisine, however, do plenty of research beforehand and talk with your vet. By boning up (no pun intended) on canine nutrition, you'll help ensure that the meals you fix your pooch not only taste good to her, but are good for her as well.

HOW MANY MEALS A DAY?

Some people say that an adult dog can get by with just one meal a day, while others say a dog should get two meals a day. Which is better?

Two meals a day are easier on the adult dog's tummy—and also on his psyche. A twice-a-day meal plan can be a real boon to the dog who spends his day alone. That's because, like people, dogs tend to get

PEOPLE FOOD FOR POOCHES

Are you looking to garnish your four-legged friend's food with some of the goodies you eat? Here are just a few good candidates for jazzing up your dog's daily fare:

- Meats: Chicken (cooked white meat or ground meat); turkey (cooked white meat or ground meat); beef (cooked lean meat or ground)
- Fruits and vegetables: Carrots (raw, cooked, or frozen; cut up fine); broccoli florets (raw, cooked, or frozen; cut up fine); Brussels sprouts (frozen); pumpkin (canned only); apples (raw and sliced); bananas (raw and sliced)
- Starch: Cooked rice (white or brown)

sleepy after they eat. Consequently, feeding in the morning can make your solitary pooch feel more like catching some z's than trashing your house. The evening feeding will get him ready for a good night's sleep.

Eating twice a day can also help prevent a very serious condition called bloat—or in vet-speak, gastric dilation volvulus. This condition is more likely to occur if a dog quickly eats a very large meal, particularly if the animal is large and deep chested. When bloat occurs, the stomach becomes so full of gas that the surrounding organs are compressed. To make matters worse, the stomach often twists at the same time compression occurs.

Symptoms of bloat—which is a life-and-death situation—include rapid abdominal expansion after a meal, restlessness, inability to lie down, and panting. If your dog exhibits such symptoms, get him to a vet immediately. His life depends on prompt expert attention.

There's one exception to the two meals a day-is-best principle: a puppy who's under four months of age. These little ones need to be fed three times every day.

HOW MUCH FOOD SHOULD I GIVE?

How do I know how much food to give my dog at each meal?

The feeding guidelines contained on dog food labels are a good starting point—but you need to recognize that they are just that: a start. Your own dog's intake will vary, depending on her age, whether she's pregnant or nursing a litter, her activity level, and where she spends most of her time. For example, a dog who competes in a canine sport such as agility needs more food than the average family pet, who in fact, probably needs less food than the manufacturers' label suggests.

Figuring out what your own dog needs may take some trial and error. If she inhales her food but is losing weight, you're clearly not feeding enough. If she's gaining weight or consistently leaves food in her dish, you're probably giving her too much. A good rule of thumb is to start with a little less than the label calls for and make adjustments from there.

24/7 FEEDING

Wouldn't life be easier for both people and dogs if we simply left food out for our dogs all the time?

The practice of leaving out dog food for your canine companion on a 24/7 basis—known among experts as "free feeding"—is unquestionably convenient for people. And it's probably fair to say that their pooches would prefer to eat whenever they felt like it, instead of waiting for their human companions to prepare them a meal. However, this is one case where opting for convenience could result in major problems for both pooches and their people.

For one thing, the practice of free feeding makes housetraining a dog much more difficult than it needs to be. A fundamental principle of teaching bathroom manners to a dog is that what goes in eventually comes out. If you know when your canine's been consuming his goodies, you can better predict when those goodies will reappear—and thus, anticipate when your four-legged friend needs a bathroom break. With free feeding, it's impossible to determine when a dog has eaten, which makes anticipating his potty times equally impossible.

Another downside to free feeding occurs because the dog loses sight of where his meals are coming from: you. By making breakfast and dinner a twice-daily ritual, your dog can see that you are his Great Provider. That realization strengthens his desire to please you, which makes for a better human-canine relationship.

Still another problem with free feeding is that the symptoms of many canine ailments include a lack of appetite. If you're feeding your dog at regular intervals, you can see immediately whether his food intake has diminished and get him the veterinary help he needs sooner rather than later. A dog whose bowl is kept perpetually filled doesn't exhibit appetite loss as quickly, which means that precious time may be lost before his human companion realizes something is wrong.

WHAT ABOUT TABLE SCRAPS?

I feel really bad giving my dog the same food day after day. Why can't I liven his menu up with a few goodies from my own table?

I suspect that your dog isn't too thrilled with getting the same food day after day, either. Although experts once displayed near-unanimity in proclaiming that dietary consistency was the key to canine health, some are now beginning to question that dictum. For example, Dr. Michael Fox, a syndicated veterinary columnist and former official of The Humane Society of the United States, confessed in one of his columns that he and his family routinely share a little bit of food from their plates with their dogs.

Fox is a veterinarian, so presumably he knows which scraps are okay for his pooches and which are not. The rest of the dog-loving populace, however, is all too likely to give their canine companions the wrong things from their plates. Moreover, unless it's done right, giving your dog tidbits from the table can encourage him to take up the obnoxious practice of begging.

Here are some guidelines for letting your dog sample food meant for people:

Don't be too literal. Giving your dog table scraps doesn't require you to give him those scraps directly from the table. A better way to share your culinary wealth is to wait until you're finished eating and then place some carefully selected leftovers into your dog's food dish. That way, he's less likely to beg for goodies while you're trying to eat.

Can the can. Once your scraps hit the garbage can, they become food that's fit only for disease-causing germs and bacteria, not for people or pooches. Moreover, giving your dog food from the garbage encourages him to try raiding the garbage can himself—a practice that can cause him tummy trouble, not to mention result in a mess that will put him in the doghouse with you.

Opt for bland. Greasy foods that are laden with spices and/or fat will wreak havoc with your dog's digestive system—and the result could be vomiting, diarrhea, or both. Better choices in table scrap cuisine are the white-meat portions of chicken and turkey (see, your dog *can* enjoy Thanksgiving dinner!), white or brown rice, and vegetables.

THE BARF DIET

I heard someone say that her dog does very well on something she called the "barf diet." Why would a diet that makes a dog vomit be good for that animal?

The BARF diet has nothing to do with vomiting. BARF is an acronym that stands for "Bones and Raw Food." The diet was developed by Australian veterinarian Ian Billinghurst, who believes that dogs' health improves if they're given food that approximates what their canine ancestors consumed in the wild.

Such food, of course, didn't come in bags or cans, and it certainly wasn't cooked. Ancient dogs—like the wolves of today—would eat the remains of animals that they or someone else had killed, and those remains would be raw. Among those remains would be raw meat, bones, and the plant residues that remained in the stomachs of the killed animals. Consequently, Billinghurst and other proponents of the BARF diet believe that the best food you can feed your dog consists of raw meat and bones, with some fresh vegetables thrown in.

People who have placed their dogs on this diet say that their dogs' overall health has improved significantly and that particularly striking enhancements can be seen in the teeth and coat of a dog who's gone the BARF route. I've seen several such dogs, both before and after their human companions placed them on the bones-and-raw-food regimen, and the results are indeed noteworthy.

But many experts—notably, veterinarians—are just as passionately against the BARF diet as the proponents are in favor of it. Many vets fear that giving a dog *any* bone, raw or cooked, will cause choking, gastrointestinal obstructions, or other emergencies. The same vets are equally worried that a dog's consumption of raw food will cause the animal to develop salmonella poisoning.

Another possible drawback to the BARF diet is that it's time consuming: People who put their pooches on this regimen must commit time not only to preparing the food but also to purchasing ingredients several times a week to ensure freshness.

If you're interested in trying the BARF diet for your canine companion, do your homework first. Check out Billinghurst's book, *Give Your Dog a Bone*, available from the author's website, www.drianbillinghurst.com. And ask your veterinarian what her opinion is. Only when you hear both sides of this ongoing dog lovers' debate can you determine what's best for your unique canine companion.

HELPING THE PUDGY POOCH

My rescue Shetland sheepdog weighs more than forty pounds and looks like an overstuffed sausage with a Lassie coat. What can I do to help him slim down?

You're right to be concerned about your not-so-svelte Sheltie. Excess weight is just as dangerous for dogs as it is for people. The pooch who carries extra poundage increases the likelihood that he'll fall victim to maladies such as diabetes, arthritis, and heart disease.

The first thing an obese dog needs to do is to visit his veterinarian, who can determine whether there's an underlying cause to the obesity.

For example, a dog who's suffering from insufficient thyroid hormone production, or hypothyroidism, will often put on lots of weight. He'll also probably have a relatively sparse coat, skin that's dry and flaky, and a lack of energy. A blood test can confirm the diagnosis, and treatment is simple: a daily pill that contains the hormone that the thyroid gland is failing to produce.

If testing enables your vet to rule out an organic cause to your dog's problem, she'll help you devise a diet and exercise plan that will help the animal to pare off the pounds. Such plans vary from dog to dog, but here are a few ideas that can help any corpulent canine:

Limit food intake—but not too much. An excessively plump pooch, like any other overweight individual, needs to cut back on the amount of food he eats, but most vets advise that such cutbacks not be too drastic. A thirty-pound dog should lose no more than one pound per month; larger dogs can take off more, while smaller dogs should lose even less.

Add some fiber. If your dog inhales his reduced rations and begs for more, adding some fiber to the diet can help. This doesn't mean dusting your dog's meal with Metamucil, though. Instead, add some fruits and vegetables to the dog's meal. Doing so will fill your dog up without adding many calories. Many dogs enjoy frozen veggies such as Brussels sprouts, green beans, and broccoli florets. Other possibilities are carrots, lettuce, canned pumpkin (not the prepared pumpkin pie filling), and sliced apple.

Pick up the pace. Dieting dogs need exercise just as much as dieting humans do. Try walking a portly pooch more often or for a longer distance. If you can find a canine spa, a swim can give your pup a good workout without straining his ligaments and joints.

TO TREAT OR NOT TO TREAT

I'm concerned about giving my dog treats. I know that many trainers suggest using them, but won't a dog who snacks put on too much weight?

Treats are a fabulous training tool. As you will see in chapters thirteen, fourteen, and fifteen, the prospect of getting a goodie can spur the most resistant dog into learning what you want to teach him. The risk, as you point out, is that such lessons will be great for his brain, but bad for his body.

To make sure your dog has an incentive to learn without giving up his sleek physique, try the following treating tactics:

Adjust his meals. If you're giving your dog some treats in order to accelerate his learning curve, cut back on the amount of food you give him at meal times. Most treat manufacturers specify how many ounces of commercial food a certain number of treats is equivalent to. Use those specs to downsize his breakfast and dinner portions.

Go low-cal. Consider bypassing commercial treats—which often are loaded with calories—for some less fattening fare. Among the low-cal treat options that many dogs love are small pieces of frozen vegetables, small pieces of apple, and pieces of rice cake. Dog food manufacturers have also developed some low-cal commercial treats you might want to try.

Wean him off the treats. Once your dog has learned a particular command, ease off on the treats you give to reward him for obeying that command. Eventually, a pat and some praise should be enough of an incentive for him to do what you've asked.

DEALING WITH THE PICKY EATER

My new dachshund is a very fussy eater. He'll eat a few bites, walk away from it for a minute, then come back and eat a bite or two more. Often he leaves food in his dish. How can I get him to eat more—and to eat faster?

There could be many reasons why your wiener dog is being picky. You may be giving him too much to eat. He may not like what he's being served. Another possibility is that he's sick. Before you call your vet, though, try a few of these taste-tempting strategies:

Reduce the rations. If your four-legged friend consistently leaves the same amount of food in his dish, try cutting what you serve him by that amount. That may be all that's needed for him to join the canine version of the Clean Plate Club.

Pack some heat. Many dogs find food to be more appealing when it's served at a warm temperature. Try putting your dog's food in the microwave (don't use a stainless steel bowl, though) for a minute or two on low heat, and see if that doesn't jump-start his appetite. If you're feeding him kibble only, a little warm water will bring out the flavor by creating some meaty-smelling gravy.

Adjust the menu. Your dog may simply not like the food he's being offered—or maybe he's just bored with it. (Wouldn't you be bored if you were saved the same thing day after day?) Try adding something new to his meal, such as a sprinkling of finely chopped raw carrot, a smidgen of cut-up frozen broccoli, or a smattering of beets. If your canine companion is eating nothing but kibble, a couple of tablespoons of canned food may perk up his palate—especially if the canned food is heated.

See if he's social. Many dogs don't like eating by themselves. If your dog stops eating in order to find out where you've gone, try sticking around while he eats. A little company may help him relax enough to enjoy his breakfast or dinner.

Don't push it. If your pooch doesn't want to eat anymore, don't force the issue. Dogs who stop eating in the middle of a meal often are coping with tender tummies. Forcing such a dog to eat could result in his vomiting not long after the meal.

Get some help. If the above measures don't work—or if your normally robust eater suddenly quits eating—put in a call to your vet. A diminished appetite may be a sign that your canine companion is sick.

EVALUATING A DOG FOOD

How can I tell if the food I'm giving my dog is right for him?

Actually, your dog will tell you everything you need to know—not that you should expect a detailed evaluation from him. The signs that your dog is eating the wrong grub for him will show up in other, more subtle ways. Here are some possible signs that your dog's food isn't as good for him as it should be:

He's porking out. If your pooch is starting to pack on some excess poundage, consider changing to a food product that's higher in protein and lower in fat content than his current regimen.

He's acting jittery. A dog who acts spazzed or is hyperactive may be getting too much protein. Try switching to a product that has a lower protein content.

He's pooping too often. A dog who's having lots of bowel movements—especially if those movements are accompanied by gas —may be eating food that has too many carbohydrates. Think about changing to a food that has a lower carb content and a higher level of protein.

His poop is loose, or stinky, or bulky. These are classic signs that a dog's having trouble digesting the nutrients in his food, which happens more often with a lower-quality product. The more digestible the nutrients are—especially the proteins—the better the food is. If your dog's stools aren't consistently firm and compact, consider switching to a higher-quality or premium product.

He's got dandruff. The pooch with flakes probably doesn't need Head and Shoulders. Instead, he probably needs a diet that has more fatty acids. Look for a food that has a higher fat content and/or fatty acids, or ask your vet about adding a fatty acid supplement to your canine companion's meals.

GIVING A BLAND DIET

My dog threw up this morning, and my vet says he needs to be on a bland diet for the next day or so. What exactly is a bland diet?

A bland diet gives a dog's human companion the opportunity to give the pooch some home-cooked food, even if the dog generally consumes commercial fare. More specifically, veterinarians prescribe bland diets to dogs whose tummies are troubled—and who manifest such troubles either by vomiting or by having diarrhea.

Such diets are simple: boiled rice mixed with either boiled hamburger or cooked white-meat chicken. Make sure the fat is skimmed off any meat that you give. Your vet will tell you how often to feed your dog this canine version of comfort food, how much to feed at any one time, and when to begin switching back to your dog's usual diet.

WATER WORKS

How much water does a dog need?

The answer to that question varies not only from dog to dog but also from activity to activity. Just like people, dogs need more water when the weather is warm or when they've engaged in vigorous exercise. Dogs whose diets consist exclusively of dry food are apt to develop more powerful thirsts than those who get canned fare.

The safest course of action to take with water and your dog is to have it available at all times during the day. Keep the water bowl full—but don't just top it off. Wash the bowl every day, and give him fresh water then. Another signal that the water needs changing: when you see stuff (for example, food residue) floating in it.

The one exception to the water-at-all-times rule is the puppy or dog who hasn't yet been housetrained. For the canine housetrainee, access to water needs to be regulated so that the dog's need to pee can be regulated. Chapter fourteen includes guidelines for giving water to the dog who's still learning basic potty protocol.

DOGGIE DINING DYNAMICS

Feeding your dog is not just a matter of *what* you feed her, but *how* you feed her. Just as you probably have definite preferences as to the way you like to eat—maybe you like to eat in front of the TV, or have Sunday morning breakfast in bed—so, too, might your new canine companion. If you make an effort to determine your dog's preferred eating environment, you could be rewarded with a dog who eats better, feels better, and behaves better than would be the case if you just fed her any old way.

For example, some dogs prefer to eat in solitary splendor, while other canine gourmands opt for eating in the midst of family activity. My own dog, Cory, seems to like a middle ground when it comes to his meals: He doesn't like to be in the middle of a lot of activity while he dines, but he doesn't like to be alone, either. So when we feed him, at least one family member sticks around. If all of the human family members want to do something else (for example, we're all watching TV in the family room downstairs), we'll simply bring Cory's dish to wherever we're all congregating. He's happy to eat his meal there.

And we're happy to cater to our canine companion's dining whims. Why? Because as a result of our showing a little consideration for Cory, he is a much less fussy eater—and a much happier dog. There are payoffs for us, too: By eating more regularly, he eliminates more regularly, which in turn makes bathroom breaks much less frustrating than they otherwise might be. In addition, by giving Cory stress-free meals, we greatly reduce postmeal tummy troubles such as vomiting, belching, and flatulence.

Although every dog is an individual—with individual dining preferences—there are some guidelines that apply to every pooch. They include:

Let him dine in peace. When your dog is eating his dinner or breakfast, don't let anyone interrupt him. That includes other human members of the family as well as other pets. For example, don't let your baby or toddler amble over to Fido's dining corner when Fido is eating in that corner. At worst, Fido will growl or snap at the perceived interloper; at best, the interloper's presence will cause Fido unnecessary stress.

Part your pets. If you live in a multipet household, feed them separately—either in different locations at the same time, or in the same location but at different times. By doing so, you'll eliminate the inevitable food fights that occur when animals try to dine together.

Let him savor his fare. Just as you enjoy lingering over a meal, so too might your dog. So give him at least fifteen minutes to eat his breakfast and dinner. Doing so will greatly reduce the likelihood of his getting an upset stomach—which in turn means you won't have to clean up any of the gross results of a tummy upset.

Do the dishes. Do you like eating off dirty dishes? Probably not—and neither does your dog. Give your dog's dish a sudsing after every meal, either by hand or in the dishwasher. And don't forget his water bowl!

CHAPTER 10

Grooming Your New Dog

NO DOG IS a totally natural beauty. Like their human companions, even the most gorgeous canines need some time to beautify their tresses or otherwise spruce themselves up. Unfortunately, though, dogs can't attend to their toilettes by themselves. They need their people to do the attending for them—in other words, to groom them.

Every dog—longhaired, shorthaired, curly coated, or silkytressed—needs regular sessions with brushes, baths, and clippers. If your dog's shedding is causing your domestic dust-bunny population to explode . . . or your dark-colored clothes are acquiring lots of little white puppy hairs . . . or your pooch's B.O. is coming between the two of you, a grooming session needs to occur sooner rather than later.

Some humans who live with dogs can't picture themselves grooming their canine companions. They picture grooming to be an undertaking that requires the sculpting of elaborate coiffures on their pooches. They envision the ornamental trimming featured by many standard poodles that compete in dog shows and feel sure that such stylings are quite beyond their own abilities. In most cases, though, such individuals are wrong. While some dogs do need the help of a professional groomer, most do just fine getting shampooed and styled by the humans they live with.

In fact, home grooming holds several important advantages for both people and pooches, including:

Saving money. A monthly professional canine grooming session can cost from $30 to well over $100, depending on the breed, the groomer, and the services you require. By doing at least some of the grooming yourself, you'll save yourself some dough.

A free health screening. The hands-on work required to groom your dog offers a great opportunity to examine him for possible health problems, such as lumps, rashes, parasites, or anything else out of the ordinary.

A chance to connect. Researchers know that just petting a dog helps both person and pooch to relax. A grooming session can offer the same benefits, magnified. Even the pros believe that grooming can be a way to connect with an animal. Who better to do the connecting with your canine companion than you?

Still, to groom your pooch properly, you need to engage in a bit of preparation. The following questions and answers should give you all the info you need to take the lead in maintaining your dog's good looks.

REQUIRED GROOMING GEAR

What equipment do I need to brush, bathe, and otherwise groom my dog?

Figuring out which items to include on your canine grooming shopping list depends, in part, on what kind of dog you have. Different dogs

Grooming time can be an enjoyable experience for both you and your dog.

with different coats need different equipment to service those coats and otherwise attend to grooming chores. However, experts generally suggest stocking up on the following items:

A brush and comb. Regular brushing and combing are crucial to keeping your canine companion comfortable, not to mention looking his best. To choose the right brush and comb for your dog, take a look at his coat. A slicker brush and a comb work well with double-coated dogs, such as rough-coated collies and Shetland sheepdogs. Dogs with long, flowing coats, such as Afghan hounds, do best with a comb and a wooden pin brush. Short-coated dogs, such as smooth dachshunds and Doberman pinschers do well with a grooming glove and rubber curry brush; a natural bristle brush is also good.

Spray bottle with water. For double-coated and long-coated dogs, an initial misting with water can make brushing go more smoothly and help prevent hair breakage. Any clean spray bottle filled with tepid water will do the trick.

Access to warm water. To properly bathe a dog, you need to have warm water at hand. That means bypassing the old-fashioned method of bathing a dog outdoors with a water-filled bucket and garden hose. Instead, plan on bathing your four-legged friend in your own bathtub—although very small dogs can be bathed in a kitchen sink.

Thick, thirsty towels. Although wet dogs invariably try to get dry by shaking themselves and rubbing their bodies against absorbent surfaces, you can ease the drying process by having some big, absorbent towels to wrap around your freshly bathed pooch. The towels can also help keep you from getting too wet and provide a nice cushion for your knees if you're bathing your dog in a floor-level bathtub.

A dog-friendly shampoo. Most groomers recommend that dog owners purchase high-quality shampoos designed specifically for dogs. The reason: Shampoos for people and lower-quality dog shampoos are too harsh for a dog's skin and coat. Groomer Aleta El-Sayed of Washington, D.C., pretests dog shampoos by pouring them onto her hands, rinsing them, and seeing how her skin feels afterward. "If my hands are still soft, I know the shampoo will be good for the dog's skin," El-Sayed says.

Lots of cotton balls. These little bits of fluff have multiple uses for dog grooming: to protect a dog's ears from soap and water, to wash and rinse the face so that soap doesn't get in the dog's eyes, and to clean a dog's bottom.

A handheld shower. Unlike their people, dogs generally can't rinse themselves; stepping under the shower and letting the water flow over their soapy bodies just isn't a viable option. Help is at hand, however, in the form of a handheld shower. These inexpensive devices, available at most department and bath stores, attach directly to the faucet and create a shower stream that you can direct onto your canine companion.

A waterproof outfit. Bathing a dog is, by definition, a very wet job.

To minimize any discomfort that results from getting wet, the human bather needs to wear an outfit that's impervious to water. Best bets are a swimsuit, or a waterproof apron over your regular clothes.

Small scissors. These are indispensable for cutting stubborn mats or tangles and for minor trims, such as the hair between the paw pads on longhaired dogs.

Nail clippers. This handy little implement, sold in several forms, keeps your canine companion's claws from becoming too long.

GIVING THE BRUSH-OFF

How often do I need to brush my collie? And how exactly do I get through all that hair?

For most breeds, a once-a-week session with brush and comb is enough to keep their skins and coats healthy and well groomed. No matter how often you brush Bowser, though, the brushing needs to be thorough to truly benefit the dog: The brush must reach not only the hair but also the skin. That's easy when grooming a shorthaired breed, such as a Boston terrier or Rhodesian Ridgeback, but a lot tougher when dealing with a longhaired breed like a golden retriever, or a double-coated breed like a collie.

Professional groomers employ special techniques to give double-coated and long-coated dogs the gentle but down-to-the-roots brushing they need. For them, the brushing method of choice is called line brushing. To line-brush your collie, here's what to do:

Have your dog lie down. The dog who reclines while being groomed is more likely to relax than his stand-at-attention counterpart. And when he lies down on his side, you'll be able to brush hard-to-reach places, such as above the tummy and on the inside flanks.

Give him a spritz. Fill your spray bottle with tepid water and mist the coat where it grows along the backbone. Don't get the hair too wet, though; the idea here is simply to dampen the coat so that brushing will be easier.

Go against the grain. Starting at the neck and working toward the tail, gently brush small sections of the coat along your dog's backbone from the skin out to the hair tip. Brush in the direction that's opposite of the way the hair grows, generally this will be toward the face. After you finish brushing the backbone hair, your dog may appear to have a Mohawk along his back.

Work line-by-line. Now that you've finished brushing the first line—that's the Mohawk—you're ready to start on the second line. With your dog continuing to lie down on his side, mist a horizontal row of the coat just below the Mohawk and brush as before. Repeat this process, line-by-line, until you've brushed the entire side. Then, have your dog turn over and brush him the same way on his other side. Make sure you also do his inner flanks, chest hair, and tail.

Check for tangles and mats. Long-coated dogs will develop tangles and tightly wadded clumps of fur—generally known as mats—in their coats. They're not only unsightly, they can also lead to discomfort and skin infections. As you brush your dog, pay special attention to prime matting areas: behind the ears, under the armpit or elbow on the front legs, and on the backs of the rear legs. To remove a mat, start by moistening it and gently working it free with your fingers, comb, or brush. If that doesn't work, you may need to cut the mat; just make sure you don't cut the dog as well.

Comb him out. The final step to brushing your long- or double-coated dog is to gently brush or comb at least some of the hair back in the direction it grows. A double-coated dog's hair will fall down on its own, except perhaps at the croup (the area just above the base of the tail); gently comb the hair there to help it lie down. A comb can also help straighten and style any long hair around the face and feathery hair on the legs. A dog with a long, silky coat will need gentle combing all over.

BRUSHING THE SHORTHAIRED DOG

My dachshund's hair is ultra-short, so he doesn't get any tangles or mats. Why do I need to brush him?

A shorthaired dog like a dachshund, Boston terrier, or Rhodesian Ridgeback doesn't need the half-hour line-brushing session that his longer-haired canine compatriots do. Nevertheless, these naturally shorthaired dogs still need the gentle skin stimulation, removal of shed hair, and overall attention that regular brushings provide.

However, brushing a shorthaired dog is usually a much simpler affair than is the case for a pooch with longer tresses. Most experts suggest a weekly going-over with a natural bristle or rubber curry brush. That will be enough to distribute the skin's natural oils throughout the coat and to pick up any hair that's been shed.

SCHEDULING SUDSING SESSIONS

People have told me that if you bathe a dog too often, you can dry out your dog's skin. Just how much bathing is too much bathing?

Baths can be as good for dogs as they are for people. A sudsing session not only cleans a dirty pooch; it also can help clear up skin problems such as mites and fungal infections.

And while dogs don't need to bathe nearly as often as their people do, the old rule about bathing a dog as infrequently as possible has gone the way of many other old wives' tales. Today, groomers agree that, at minimum, a monthly bath is needed to keep a dog's coat and skin in top condition and that frequent bathing won't hurt the dog's coat or skin. The key is to pick the right shampoo: A product meant specifically for dogs will keep the coat and skin from drying out.

BATHING 101

I just adopted my dog from an animal shelter, and she really stinks. But I've never given a dog a bath before. Just what do I do?

Bathing a dog can seem daunting until you do it the first time. Here's how to do the job for maximum impact but minimum hassle:

Brush up beforehand. Before you start, make sure your dog is thoroughly brushed and is free of mats and tangles. This prebath bristle session is especially important for longhaired and double-coated dogs. Failure to brush such dogs before a trip to the tub will cause their wet hair to bond together in clumps that look like dreadlocks. Such clumps are very difficult to brush out when they dry.

Cotton to him. Place a cotton ball in each ear to protect it from water. For dogs, water in the ear is very uncomfortable.

Water down the shampoo. Many groomers suggest adding three or four units of water to every unit of shampoo you plan to use. The reason: Watering down the shampoo helps it to lather and rinse more easily.

Put him in the tub. If you're lucky, your dog will go into the tub on his own; if not, lift him carefully and put him there. Lay down a bath mat beforehand to keep his feet steady.

Keep a steady hand. If your dog doesn't yet appreciate the pleasures of bathing, keep a steady hand on him while he's in the tub. That bit of restraint may prevent him from hopping out. And just in case he does make it out of the tub, make sure your bathroom door is closed, so that he doesn't go running through the house before the bath is done.

Water him down. With a handheld shower attachment, pour warm water over your dog, making sure the water goes all the way down to the skin. Start at the top of his head and neck, then wet the length of his backbone. After that, water the sides, chest, legs, and tail.

Lather him up. Apply enough diluted shampoo to work up a lather all over the dog's body, but don't go overboard with the suds. If you see billowy clouds of suds in the tub or on your pooch, you're laying the lather on too thick.

Tend the tender places. Ears and faces need special attention during your dog's bath. Use a damp cotton ball to wipe the face and clean the ears. If your dog's ears are floppy, apply a canine ear-cleaning solution inside the earflap, then lower the flap and massage the ear.

Rinse, rinse, rinse. After you've soaped your pooch completely, use the handheld shower attachment to rinse him off. Rinse from front to back and top to bottom—the same order in which you performed the initial dousing—and keep doing so for at least five minutes, or until the rinse water runs clear, whichever comes last. A less-than-thorough rinse will leave the dog's skin dry, flaky, and itchy.

Help him dry off. A couple of big, thick towels applied to your sparkling clean pooch will help soak up excess water. Don't rub, though; that could cause the coat to tangle. Instead, gently blot the excess water from the coat and skin. Then, let your dog indulge in an after-bath running frenzy—after which you can towel him some more, or use a blow-dryer if he tolerates it.

Get him in style. Most dogs need a post-bath brushing to style their tresses, but the timing of that brushing depends on the type of coat he has. Dogs with kinky, long, or double coats do better with damp brushing than with their coats dry. However, curly coats, such as the one sported by the curly-coated retriever, do better with a dry-hair brushing.

THE ART OF THE PEDICURE

How do I trim my dog's toenails?

Although tending your dog's toenails is an essential part of the grooming process, many people dread doing the job, or even skip it altogether. That omission may reduce hassles over the short term, but it will cause your dog considerable pain later. That's because toenails allowed to grow too long can throw a dog's feet out of alignment the same way that stiletto heels affect women's feet and balance.

Experts recommend keeping your dog's toenails short enough to be off the ground when he's standing still. Dewclaws (the nails that are found higher up on the leg near the ankle) should be kept sufficiently short to prevent their curving back into the skin of the leg. Here's how to do the job:

Have your dog relax. Put your four-legged friend in either a sitting or reclining position—whichever is more relaxing for him, while also being reasonably easy for you to reach.

Look for the quick. A dog's toenail has a blood vessel inside that runs almost to the end of the nail. If your dog's nails are light in color, you can see the quick; it's the pink area inside the nail. Dark nails are more problematic, because the quick can't be seen; you need to estimate where the quick is.

Trim just a bit. Pick up the clippers, gently squeeze the paw to extend the nails a bit, and place the clippers around the very end of one nail. Squeeze the clippers quickly to trim off the nail tip. Continue trimming a little at a time until you see the black dot in the center of the trimmed nail. The black dot signals the start of the quick.

If there's blood, don't panic. Despite your best efforts, you may trim off too much nail and hit the quick—and when that happens, the nail will bleed. To stop the bleeding, just apply some styptic powder (available in pharmacies) or ordinary baking flour to the nail. The bleeding will stop very quickly. Above all, don't fuss too much, or your dog will sense that you're upset—and such distress can be contagious!

THE POOCH WHO HATES PEDICURES

My dog can't stand to have his nails trimmed. What can I do?

No matter how much your canine companion hates getting a pedicure, it's important to keep his nails trimmed short. A dog with overly long nails suffers from a lack of balance when he walks, much like a woman who's teetering around in three-inch high heels.

If your dog hates having his nails trimmed, a little bribery and a lot of patience can get the job done, albeit at a much slower pace than with a dog who tolerates his pedicures. Wait till your dog's relaxed. Have some treats on hand, and then pick up one of your dog's paws. Trim just one nail—and then end the session for the day. Give your dog a treat.

Once your dog tolerates getting one nail trimmed per day, start adding a second nail to the daily regimen—again using treats to sweeten the process. Taken slowly, even a clipper-phobic dog may learn to tolerate a session with the hated instrument.

Some experts believe that the most common type of pet nail clippers—called guillotine clippers—are too dull to cut the nail efficiently and put too much pressure on the nail. Such pressure can be painful to your pooch and, in fact, may be at the root of his nail-trimming phobia. Some less painful alternatives to guillotine clippers are scissor clippers and grinders. Scissor clippers are stronger and sharper and tend to pinch the nail less. A grinder is a cordless, rechargeable device originally intended for precision drilling, sanding, shaping, and detailing of wood and other building materials. Grinders are available at home improvement stores and the home improvement departments of stores such as Wal-Mart and Sears.

HELP FOR THE GROOM-O-PHOBE

My golden retriever hates getting groomed—brushing, blow-drying, you name it. How can I help him overcome his phobia and keep his coat in decent condition?

Although grooming is supposed to be relaxing for dog and human alike, sometimes the task is anything but. Too many dogs and their people find a brush-and-suds session to be more of a human–canine wrestling match than a chance to chill out, reconnect, and help Fido look his best. Still, there are ways to overcome a dog's antipathy for grooming—and they all center on helping the animal to relax.

For example, Susan Sholar of the California School of Dog Grooming suggests using a dog treat to persuade a brush-hating dog to cooperate—and then brushing just a little bit at a time. "Brush your dog for five minutes, then give him a treat," she suggests. Keep doing this in five-minute increments. Once he learns that after five minutes of brushing he'll get a goodie, he'll look forward to being brushed.

If your dog hates the blow-dryer, try persuading him to get acquainted with the appliance. Call him over to sniff the dryer, and give him a treat when he does so. After that, turn on the dryer with the appliance lying on the floor and again encourage him to check the dryer out. If he does, another treat is in order.

Above all, don't point the dryer at your dog until he's comfortable with the contraption. Once that happens, start at the lowest temperature setting and begin drying the dog's rear end. "That way," says Sholar, "the dog can watch the dryer and feel what it's doing."

To help a dog relax even more during a brushing or pedicure, try pairing the session with time in front of the television. Both people and pooches tend to relax when they share some tube time—and that relaxation can help a grooming session go more smoothly.

DEALING WITH FURRY FEET

I try to keep my cocker-poo looking nice, but she's got a lot of hair growing out from her toes and between her paw pads. What, if anything, should I do about such furry feet?

You should get rid of as much of that fur as possible. With a pair of baby scissors, carefully trim the hair that grows from the paws so that the fur follows the shape of the foot. Then, turn the paw over and clip the hair down to the level of the paw pad. By doing so, you'll limit the likelihood that your dog will get pebbles, pollen, or other ground-level debris caught in her feet. You'll also reduce the likelihood that she'll slip and fall on uncarpeted floors.

A SUMMER HAIRCUT

I live in Florida, and the temperature gets terribly high (with humidity to match!) during the summer. Wouldn't shaving my golden retriever's fur help him stay cooler?

A summer shave-down won't help your dog endure the summer's heat; in fact, a Bowser buzz-cut may add to his discomfort. That's because dogs, like people, are susceptible to sunburn (and skin cancer!), if their skins are exposed to the sun's deadly rays. Making matters worse is the fact that when the hair grows back in, it might cause your dog's skin to itch.

To keep your golden cool and comfy, keep him indoors—especially during the hottest time of day—and keep the indoor temperature as comfortable for him as you do for yourself. Make sure, too, that fresh water is always available. Those simple steps will do much more than shaving to help your canine companion take his summer in stride.

DOGGIE DENTAL CARE

My veterinarian has told me that I need to brush my dog's teeth! Why? And, assuming she'll even let me do it, exactly how do I give my dog a tooth-brushing?

Your vet is absolutely right to recommend that you pay attention to your pooch's choppers. According to the American Veterinary Dental Society, more than eighty percent of dogs show signs of gum disease by the tender age of three. Such disease, if left unchecked, can cause not only doggie bad breath but also the separation of the tooth from the gum. Even worse is the possibility that the bacteria can cause vital organs such as the heart, lungs, liver, and kidneys to contract dangerous bacterial infections. Such infections can lead to serious organ damage—or even death.

Prevention of canine gum problems and other dental diseases starts at home with daily brushings of your dog's teeth, or at least regular brushing sessions. Frequent brushings do the same things for your dog's teeth that they do for yours: They remove the mixture of food particles, saliva, minerals, and bacteria that form a coating of plaque on the teeth. The plaque is the breeding ground for the bacteria that can eventually cause those life-threatening infections.

Brushing your dog's teeth need not be difficult. Here's what experts suggest you do:

Get the right brush and toothpaste. A child's toothbrush will have bristles that are sufficiently soft to clean the teeth and gums without irritating them. Don't put human toothpaste on that brush, though; it could upset your animal friend's stomach. Instead, stick with toothpastes made especially for dogs. Such toothpastes won't leave your dog with the minty-fresh breath that manufacturers of human toothpastes extol—among the available flavors are peanut butter and chicken—but they will do the truly important job of forestalling a plaque attack.

Start slow. Don't feel that you have to start wielding the toothbrush immediately. Finger brushes, or even gauze wrapped around your finger, that gently rub the teeth and gums can help your pooch get accustomed to having her mouth area worked with.

Make it a habit. Be consistent about when you brush your dog's teeth. Every day at the same time each day is best.

Keep her mouth shut. Opening the mouth isn't necessary to brush your canine's canines. Simply lift your dog's lips and brush the outer surfaces of the teeth. The dog's own tongue can keep the inner surfaces clean.

Give an incentive. If your dog can expect something nice to happen right after a brushing, she's much more likely to tolerate the procedure. Good rewards include a walk or play session. Don't give her a treat, though: Doing so defeats the purpose of brushing.

WHEN HOME GROOMING DOESN'T CUT IT

Alas, sometimes home grooming—despite its advantages—just doesn't do the job. Some dogs are so rambunctious that grooming them is more like a wrestling match than a bonding session. Other dogs live with people who simply don't have the time to groom their pooches thoroughly, or who are phobic about certain tasks. Dogs can be phobic, too: They may be unable to abide having their nails trimmed and their coats shampooed by amateurs like yourself. And, finally, there are some dogs who are perfectly happy to be groomed at home but whose coats need the touch of a pro.

If any of these descriptions resemble you or your canine companion, don't despair. It's not hard to find a professional groomer, if you know what to do. Here's what the pros suggest:

Start with your vet. Your veterinarian is the best person to start with in your search for a groomer. For one thing, many veterinary practices keep groomers on staff—which can make your search gratifyingly short. But even if that's not the case with your vet, she's still likely to know which groomers would be best for your particular pooch.

Ask around. Just as most people love to share the names of their own hairdressers, they're equally happy to share the names of those who tend their dogs' tresses. If you're in a training class, a dog park, or even just out on the street, don't be afraid to query a person whose dog sports a coiffure that you like.

Chat up the groomer. Once you've gotten a few names of grooming pros, pick up the phone and call for a chat. A ten-minute call can yield information about prices, cancellation policies, business volume, and emergency procedures. A groomer who answers all such questions to your liking is worth investigating further.

Visit the shop. If you like what you've heard from a groomer so far, ask if you can pay her shop a visit. Once you're there, take a good look around. The shop should be reasonably clean (a little hair on the floor is to be expected, huge piles of hair are not) and not have overwhelming smells (the fragrance of dog shampoo is fine; the pungent aroma of doggie accidents is not). Look, too, at how the groomer and her colleagues interact with their canine clients.

If, after taking these steps, the groomer and her shop check out, you're ready to book a get-acquainted appointment for your canine companion.

CHAPTER 11

Exercising Your New Dog

THANKS TO THE exhortations of doctors—not to mention countless pages of print devoted to the subject—most people now understand the importance of getting themselves into shape and staying that way. We realize that regular exercise gives our bodies more staying power: healthier hearts, stronger bones and muscles, and better-working digestive systems. Regular workouts help us control our weight, too.

Interestingly enough, our canine companions can benefit from exercise even more than we humans do. That's because, in addition to the physical benefits that working out gives to pooches and people alike, exercise brings solid behavioral benefits to our dogs.

The proof of this principle is right here in my own home, with my Shetland sheepdog Cory. Like most Shelties, Cory has a tendency to bark way more often than my husband, daughter, and I like. Even worse is the fact that he's often at his most talkative during particularly inconvenient times for us, such as when we're answering the door or telephone. But where other families would simply yell at their noisy pooch, we've learned a better way to help Cory quiet down: giving him some exercise.

Sometimes that exercise takes the form of a Frisbee session in our backyard. Other times, one of us will take him for a long, brisk walk. And on still other occasions, we'll chase him around the house in a psuedo-attempt to take his favorite toy of the moment (currently a white stuffed kitty cat that meows when squeezed) away from him. Cory particularly loves these keep-away sessions and keeps up a blistering pace.

After any of these activities, Cory is panting and wants to do nothing more than chill. At such times, he's much less likely to bark—even if the phone rings or the doorbell chimes.

My family's not alone in finding that exercise can help control a dog's undesirable behavior. Animal behaviorists are quick to prescribe daily exercise plans to combat any one of several doggie behavior challenges. Barking dogs, overactive dogs, destructive dogs, and anxious dogs all benefit from regular physical activity.

Staying in shape is just as important for your dog as it is for you!

The question is, what kind of activity? The answer depends in part on your dog, your schedule, and each of your individual preferences. Still, there are some forms of exercise that any dog can enjoy and benefit from. These include:

- Walking, if done at a fairly brisk pace and without stopping to sniff and anoint each and every vertical surface;
- Jogging, once a dog reaches adulthood;
- Swimming, under supervision so that a dog can exit the pool or pond when he gets tired;
- Canine sports, such as agility and flyball, that help a dog use his mind as well as his body;
- Soccer—albeit a modified form from the human version of the sport. Simply kicking a soccer ball around the yard will prompt many dogs to chase it, making for a great workout.

But just as some people prefer jogging while others would rather ride a bike, dogs have definite exercise preferences, too. Often, such preferences depend on what the dog has been bred to do. For example, a golden retriever would probably enjoy playing fetch (in other words, a retrieving game) till he dropped. But a malamute, who's bred to pull a sled, would probably much rather play tug-of-war.

Here are some ideas for breed-specific exercises and activities:

- Herding dogs, such as Shelties, collies, German shepherds, Old English sheepdogs, and corgis, enjoy chase games and retrieving games, both of which appeal to their herding roots. They may also be avid soccer players. And most relish the chance to try actual herding, with real live sheep.
- Sporting dogs, such as golden retrievers and Labrador retrievers, and most hounds, such as dachshunds, enjoy retrieving games. They may also enjoy field trials, which are events conducted by dog clubs that are designed to simulate hunting situations.

- Terriers, such as Jack Russells, and many herding dogs excel at agility training.
- Working dogs, such as Rottweilers, and other large-shouldered dogs may enjoy pulling-type games or a new canine sport called carting, in which dogs pull carts in competition.

The following questions and answers provide more details on various canine sports and help solve specific exercise problems that you and your canine companion might encounter.

WHEN TO START EXERCISING

Can I start exercising my new puppy right away?

That depends on what you mean by "exercise" and "right away." If you're talking about a puppy under four months of age, gentle games of fetch or hide-and-seek or a low-key stroll are sufficient; anything more strenuous might put too much strain on a canine youngster's soft, growing bones and ligaments. You also should confine your frolicking to soft surfaces, such as dirt, carpet, or grass, to provide further cushioning for your growing pooch.

HOW LONG A WALK?

How much walking does a dog need to do each day to get enough exercise?

There's no single answer to this question; again, it all depends upon the dog's size, age, and personality. As a general rule, twenty minutes of brisk walking—in other words, not a leisurely stroll in which every vertical surface gets a sniff and a squirt—every day is a good goal to work toward and to maintain.

CANINE SPORTS 101

I keep hearing about canine sports such as agility and flyball, but I don't know anything about them, much less how to get my dog into them. Where do I start?

Here's a quick introduction to some popular canine sports. See Table 11.1 for contact information:

Agility is probably the fastest-growing canine sport in the United States. In this sport, human handlers guide dogs through obstacle courses that consist of hurdles, teeter-totters, tunnels, balance beams, and similar apparatus. Although terriers, such as Jack Russells, and herding breeds, such as corgis, Border collies, and Shelties, are naturals at this sport, almost any breed can learn it.

Flyball is a relay race that requires teams of dogs to catch tennis balls that have been released from a spring-loaded launcher. The dogs then race over hurdles and eventually back to the starting line, where the next dogs on the teams start their runs. The herding breeds often excel at this sport, too, but any dog can try it.

Tracking, according to the American Kennel Club's website at www.akc.org, "is a vigorous, non-competitive outdoor sport . . . [that] demonstrates the dog's ability to recognize and follow human scent." The AKC tests dogs' tracking abilities and awards titles based on the distance the dog is able to track and the age of the tracks themselves. Not surprisingly, it's a natural for hounds, such as basset hounds and bloodhounds, but other types of dogs enjoy it, too.

Field trials allow a dog to perform tracking, pointing, and retrieval of a quarry in environments that simulate the hunting conditions for which field dogs were originally bred. In such trials, dogs compete against each other for points and titles. A related set of events are hunting tests, which are noncompetitive events designed to test an individual dog's ability to deal with hunting situations. If the dog passes the test, he wins a title. Both types of events are designed specifically for sporting breeds, although one type of test, the Earthdog Test, is designed for low-to-ground dogs, such as dachshunds and various terriers.

Herding is exactly what it sounds like: a set of tests and trials designed to assess your canine companion's ability to move livestock—sheep, ducks, turkeys, or cattle—from one place to another under your direction. This sport is a lot of fun for all herding breeds (although not every individual herding-breed dog enjoys it), but also other breeds such as Rottweilers, Samoyeds, and others. Breed eligibility depends on the herding organization that you work with.

Carting, also known as drafting, provides recreation and competition for dogs who were originally bred to pull carts or sleds. Among the breeds most suited to carting are Bernese mountain dogs, Newfoundlands, and Rottweilers—although the Capital Canine Carting Club of Texas reports that breeds as small as papillons have been trained to pull. (The paps pull a specially modified child's toy dump truck). The Newfoundland and Bernese mountain dog clubs are among those that sponsor carting tests that convey titles on those dogs that pass, but there are no national, all-breed titles at present.

CANINE WORKOUTS FOR TIME-CHALLENGED HUMANS

I'd love to take my corgi herding or have her do agility, but I just don't have the time! How do I get her the exercise she needs—and enjoys?

Your corgi won't mind never having seen a sheep or a duck or an agility course, as long as you find some other way to exercise her body and her mind. Because corgis are herding dogs, they adore exercise that involves chasing and fetching. An indoor game of keep-away or an

TABLE 11.1 ON-LINE CANINE SPORTS CONTACTS

Sport	Organization	Address or Website
Agility	American Kennel Club	www.akc.org
	North American Dog Agility Council	www.nadac.com
	United States Dog Agility Association	www.usdaa.com
	United Kennel Club	www.ukc.org
Flyball	North American Flyball Association	www.flyball.com
Tracking	American Kennel Club	www.akc.org
Field Trials	American Kennel Club	www.akc.org
Herding	American Kennel Club	www.akc.org
	American Herding Breeds Association	www.ahba-herding.org
	U.S. Border Collie Handlers Association	www.border-collie.org
	Australian Shepherd Club of America	www.asca.org
Carting	Capital Canine Carting Club	www.angelfire.com/tx2/ CCCC/homepage.html

outdoor game of doggie-style soccer or fetch will help her get in touch with her herding roots without your needing to find any livestock or agility gear. Doing those activities every few days, along with one or two daily walks of twenty minutes or so, should keep your little herder happy.

MOVING THE CANINE COUCH POTATO

My dachshund is quite overweight and generally prefers napping on the sofa to going for a walk (much less do anything really active!). How can I get him moving enough to pare off some of his poundage?

You're right to want to encourage your portly pooch to get some exercise. Excess weight forces a dog's heart and lungs to work harder, interferes with digestion and other crucial bodily functions, and strains the bones, muscles, and joints. Getting rid of your canine companion's excess baggage calls for the same strategy that you would employ for yourself: Eat less and exercise more.

However, a slow-moving, overweight dog may suffer from more than simply too many goodies coupled with too little exercise. Excess weight combined with lethargy can also be symptomatic of one or more health problems, such as hypothyroidism. This condition occurs when the thyroid gland fails to produce enough thyroid hormone for the dog's body to function properly—and lack of interest in exercising is often the first solid indicator that a dog suffers from this condition. Fortunately, hypothyroidism can be easily cured with a daily regimen of pills that contain synthetic thyroid hormone.

Consequently, if your not-so-pleasingly-plump wiener dog shows little interest in throwing his weight around, a trip to the veterinarian is in order. Your vet can draw a sample of your dog's blood that, when analyzed, will confirm whether the thyroid hormone is the culprit behind your dog's corpulence and lethargy.

If your vet doesn't uncover any underlying causes of your dog's couch-potato tendencies, it's time to get him moving, albeit slowly. Start with gentle walks for increasingly longer distances (perhaps with some low-calorie treats for encouragement), and work up to regular jaunts that are done at a brisker pace. Consider, too, the value of having buddies; see whether your dog perks up when taken to a dog park or even for visits with a canine playmate. Swimming can be a great activity for the overweight dog, because it calls for vigorous exercise that doesn't stress the joints.

At the same time you're working to raise the fitness level of your portly pooch, work with your vet to map out an appropriate reducing diet for your dog—and stick with it.

AN INDOOR WORKOUT

How can I give my dog some exercise when it's cold or rainy outside?

Simple: Move the workout indoors. Unless your dog is the size of a young horse, he won't mind taking the action inside.

In fact, your pooch can show you what kind of indoor exercise he likes. For example, my Cory likes to play keep-away. He'll pick up his favorite toy and shove it into my hip, place it on my chair, or set it at my feet. I'll reach down to pick up the toy, but Cory will grab it first—and start running away with it. My job is to stop whatever I'm doing and chase him around the house in a vain attempt to catch him and take the toy away. We keep this up for ten or fifteen minutes. This game gives us both a nice little aerobic workout.

Other dogs prefer to play hide-and-seek (with either you or a toy as the object that's hidden), fetch, or other games. Let your own particular pooch guide your indoor activities, and you may be surprised at how much fun you can both have inside.

ENCOURAGING NONSTOP WALKING

I'd love to go jogging with my new dog while he's on his leash, but he wants to sniff and squirt on just about every vertical surface we encounter. How can I stop this behavior?

I've literally felt the pain you must encounter when you try to combine your own fitness regimen with some sort of workout for your dog. If I let him, my own dog, Cory, would take multiple sniff-and-squirt breaks during our daily power walks. However, after a certain point in the walk, I don't let him stop to smell the flowers or anything else. You can do the same with your dog. Here's how:

Give some initial sniff time. If you're combining your power walk with your pooch's bathroom break, let him take his time and sniff the ground for a block or so into your jaunt. He needs to check things out at ground level in order to find the right place to pee. (Finding just the right place to do the deed seems to be a very big deal for some dogs.) Once he's opened his floodgates, though, your walk or jog can begin in earnest.

Tell him what's happening. Once his sniff-and-squirt time is over, tell him so. I tell Cory, "OK, boy, it's time for our constitutional" —and emphasize the latter word. Your dog won't understand what you're saying at first. Eventually, though, he will get the message, especially if you pair it with the next step.

Keep moving. Once you've told your four-legged friend that it's time for your joint workout, back up your words with action. If he wants to stop and sniff, keep moving—and as you do, tell him, "No, Fido, this is our constitutional (or whatever word you want to use)." He can't stop for very long if you're on the move. And eventually, once he hears the word, he'll associate it with the behavior you expect of him.

Slow down toward the end. After you've been jogging or power walking together for about twenty minutes, slow down. Not only will easing your pace give the two of you a chance to cool down —an important element in both human and canine exercise— but it will also give your canine companion a chance to do some last-minute sniffing and squirting.

USING EXERCISE TO SOLVE BEHAVIOR PROBLEMS

How can exercise solve a dog's behavior problems? Are there specific exercises for specific problems, or is there some other way that being active helps?

Experts routinely prescribe exercise for dogs with all kinds of bad behavioral habits. They don't suggest specific activities, though. Instead, they schedule canine clients' workouts at the times when the dog is most likely to exhibit the undesired behavior.

Suppose your canine companion is biting or mouthing you when you come home from work. Naturally, you try to avoid those flashing canine teeth, but your evasive maneuvers seem to cause the dog's behavior to worsen. A behaviorist might surmise that your pooch is simply trying to get your attention and that exercise is a way to give the dog what he wants and also end the biting behavior. Consequently, taking your dog for a brisk walk and spending a few minutes playing with him as soon as you arrive home might go a long way toward bypassing your dog's oral greeting.

Exercise is particularly helpful in alleviating a dog's anxiety. For example, if you're a woman and your dog becomes jealous when your new boyfriend visits, a behaviorist might suggest that a dog get some exercise right before the boyfriend is scheduled to come over. The activity itself helps the dog to become mellower—and in addition, the establishment of a new routine can alleviate his anxiety. The dog who gets some exercise and fun time with his human companion at a time when he's likely to be agitated will soon start replacing his anxiety with pleasurable anticipation. In other words, he'll forget to be anxious.

TO TUG OR NOT TO TUG

I have a dog who loves nothing better than to play tug-of-war. But I've read that playing tug is a bad idea, that it can cause a dog to be more aggressive. Are there any circumstances under which playing tug-of-war is okay?

I used to worry about playing tug-of-war with my dog, too; in fact I would feel guilty about doing so. I'd taken to heart experts' warnings that this traditional human-to-canine activity may bring out the Mr.

Hyde in a canine Dr. Jekyll. The fact that my dog, Cory, is a gentle, reserved Sheltie did little to allay my fears.

But according to some experts, I may actually boost my shy Sheltie's self-confidence when I give in to his pleas to pull. One trainer, the late Robin Kovary of New York City, told me, "For a shy dog, tug-of-war can actually help if it's done properly. By playing tug-of-war, you're telling a shy dog that it needn't be afraid, that it can interact with you without being worried about severe consequences."

Other trainers agree that playing tug-of-war is fine—if you adhere to the following guidelines:

Control when the game starts. Because tug-of-war is a contest in which the two tuggers vie for dominance over each other, it's important to make sure your dog knows that eventually you, not he, will win. One way to do this is to control when the game starts: Make sure, for example, that your pooch earns the privilege of playing. Have him sit or lie down on your command before you start the game. (Instructions on how to teach your dog these and other commands are in chapter fifteen.)

Control when the game ends. Another way to remind your canine companion that you are in control of all tugging games is to be the player who decides when the game ends. Have your dog drop the tugged object when you are ready to call it quits—and praise him when he does. (More on teaching your dog to drop an object appears in chapter fifteen.)

Use the right toy. Trainers warn people to use a rope toy or plastic pulling toy for tugging sessions—not a shoe, sock, or part of your person. The reason: The dog won't be able to understand why it's okay to tug those objects but not be able play with them (or chew them!) at other times.

EXERCISE DOS AND DON'TS

No matter what exercise you choose for your dog, it's important to make sure that your canine companion has a safe, comfortable work-out. Here are some suggestions to get your dog's exercise program off to a good start:

Do consult your vet. Before starting any fitness regimen, talk with your vet to see what kind of exercise is best for your particular pooch's age, size, and health condition.

Don't do too much too soon. Just as human fitness newcomers should take their time and build their stamina gradually, so should their canine counterparts.

Do keep cool. Veterinarians suggest limiting exercise during the hottest parts of the day, particularly during early summer, in order to prevent heat stroke, which can be fatal.

Don't forget water. Both human and canine athletes need plenty of water during a workout in order to prevent dehydration.

Do keep safety in mind. Pick places to exercise that aren't danger-ous to either dog or owner. Avoid areas near heavily traveled roads, or places that are too deserted.

CHAPTER 12

Socializing Your New Dog

IF YOUR DOG'S sole companions are you and other members of your household, you may be jeopardizing his emotional health and well-being.

Even if you feed your four-legged friend gourmet fare, give him the cushiest bed imaginable, spend all your spare time with him, and otherwise do your best to ensure that he's the most pampered of pooches, he's still going to be missing something that's crucial to his being a well-adjusted canine. That "something" is a social life.

A dog's social life doesn't consist of a canine version of a Palm Pilot in which he balances a burgeoning calendar of parties and other engagements. And as his social director, you are not required to overprogram him into a dizzying array of activities (any more than the social life of a human child should require a parent to engage in similar balancing acts). For the dog, a social life simply means consistently exposing him to people, pets, and places outside the four walls of his family home. This ongoing exposure is what experts call socialization

The well-adjusted dog has friends outside his human family.

—and it's as important to a dog's well-being as sheltering, feeding, and training him.

A dog who's been socialized can take the unexpected in stride. He can deal with new experiences without falling apart. Visitors to his home, walks in crowds, or trips in the car don't faze him. He's a confident animal who's easy to live with.

By contrast, the unsocialized dog can be extremely difficult and even dangerous to live with. The pooch who hasn't had early and consistent exposure to new people, places, and situations probably will be much more fearful than his socialized counterpart, simply because he hasn't had a chance to learn that a new experience is not necessarily a bad experience.

Some fearful dogs express their apprehension over the unfamiliar by hiding in a corner or under a piece of furniture. Others seem to decide that the best defense is a good offense and react by growling, snarling, or even biting. They become aggressive. In fact, many cases of growling, snarling, or biting are not instigated by nasty or combative dogs, but by dogs who are fearful—or simply don't know any better. For that reason alone, it behooves the conscientious guardian to make sure that her canine companion has a rich social life. That way, the dog will learn that there's little in his world that he needs to be afraid of. Consistent socialization conveys that lesson continuously, over the dog's entire lifetime.

Ideally, the socialization process begins before you bring your puppy home. As early as three weeks of age, a puppy begins to learn how to behave with his littermates and with his mother, who all teach him basic canine good manners. These early lessons, which continue until the puppy is about seven weeks old and weaned from his mother, lay the foundation necessary for a puppy to learn from human beings later on. Conversely, if a puppy is removed from his mother and littermates before seven weeks of age, he may have trouble being trained and trouble relating well to people for the rest of his life.

Of course, the mama dog isn't a young puppy's only teacher. A good breeder plays a leading role in a canine youngster's early socialization process. Something as simple as a car ride to the veterinarian's for that first round of puppy shots is a stimulating experience for a puppy and provides a good introduction to the world outside the breeder's home.

The world inside the breeder's home is crucial, too. If your puppy and his littermates are being raised in an outdoor kennel, he may not get the time with people that he needs to become an ideal canine companion. Conversely, a puppy who's raised indoors with a breeder and her family gets plenty of exposure to people and becomes accustomed to a family atmosphere—particularly handling by children. Not surprisingly, the pup who's raised indoors is more likely to enjoy human company than the kenneled canine youngster.

Once you get your puppy home, you can—and should—continue the socialization process. A day or so after your little one arrives home, start having people over to meet him and take him around your neighborhood. Take him to local parks and playgrounds and to other local facilities to help him get comfortable with everyday sights, sounds, and happenings.

Sooner or later, your puppy is bound to confront something that startles or frightens him. The way you respond to that situation is extremely important. Don't coddle him; if you croon, "There, there" to your little darling, you're telling him that he *should* be afraid. By soothing him, you're reinforcing his fear and setting him up to be scared every time he sees whatever it is that gives him the willies.

Instead of soothing your skittish pup, convince him that he can be brave. Encourage him and tell him that he doesn't need to be afraid. And when he begins to walk past whatever's spooking him, praise him for his bravery. To this day, I tell my dog, Cory, what a brave boy he is whenever we encounter something that scares him. Just hearing the words *brave boy* seems to give him the courage he needs to walk calmly past the scary object.

Unfortunately, not every dog has had the benefit of being socialized during puppyhood. In fact, a lot of adult dogs with behavioral problems were once puppies who missed out on such experiences. If you've adopted such a dog, you'll have to help him play catch-up and begin to introduce him to what he should have encountered as a puppy. But because his fears may be more entrenched, you may need to set a slower pace than you would for a pup. Here are some things you can try if your adult dog needs remedial socialization:

Establish a routine. Feed, walk, and play with your dog at the same time every day. This will give him feelings of structure and predictability, which will help to build his confidence.

Let your dog be the decision maker. If you're introducing your dog to new people or taking him to someplace different and he becomes stressed or upset, stop immediately—but try again at another time.

Offer options. When your dog becomes stressed over something you can't control—for example, thunder—show him that he doesn't have to be scared. Play with him or do something else to divert his attention from whatever is causing him to feel afraid.

SOCIALIZING AND SHOTS

I want to be able to socialize my new puppy, but my vet has told me that I cannot take her anywhere until she's had all her shots. How can I socialize her if I can't take her out of the house?

Your veterinarian makes an important point. Until puppies have had all of their shots—usually at about sixteen weeks of age—they're vulnerable to contracting highly contagious and all-too-often fatal diseases like distemper and parvovirus. Consequently, veterinarians often tell their clients to refrain from taking their puppies out in public. Keeping Fido under wraps is the easiest method of keeping him out of harm's way.

The trouble is, keeping Fido inside makes socialization very difficult. It's tough to introduce a puppy to the world when you're not able to take the puppy out in it. Fortunately, this isn't an either-or situation. You can socialize your little one without putting him at undue risk. Here's how:

Bring the world to your pup. If you hesitate to take your dog outside, bring some of that outside world to him. Invite people and well-behaved pooches over to your home to play with your new family member. You can also bring your puppy to their homes. Either way, though, make sure that those other pooches are healthy and fully immunized.

Go where no dog has gone before. There are plenty of places you can bring your new canine companion without putting him in harm's way. Basically, any place at which humans congregate is probably okay—as long as dogs haven't congregated there as well.

Bypass doggie hot spots. The only places that you and your puppy need to avoid are those where dogs you don't know tend to congregate. Such places include pet stores, dog parks, and other public places that are dog-friendly.

Pick him up. Sometimes, if you're not sure whether a place is safe for your puppy, the best thing to do is to just carry him. Let him view the world from your entirely safe lap or the comfort of your arms, and he'll be both socialized and safe.

TOOTHY TALES

My four-month-old puppy is nipping at my arm and hand. How do I get her to stop?

The short answer to this question is simple: Tell her.

That said, it's important to realize that four-month-old puppies usually don't bite or nip out of meanness or aggressiveness. They generally put the bite on a playmate for one of two reasons.

For one thing, a four-month-old dog may well be in the process of losing her baby teeth as her grown-up choppers emerge. This is a perfectly normal process, but it's painful for the pup. The new teeth are putting pressure on her gums; consequently, she's in some pain. To relieve her discomfort, she instinctively bites down on whatever's available—even if that available something is a human arm.

Another reason that a puppy puts some teeth into her interactions with people is that she's playing. Young puppies often nip when they play with their littermates. Usually, those littermates—not to mention the mama dog—discipline the puppy who bites too hard. However, some pups take a while to learn this lesson. And if a pup is taken from her litter too soon (before seven weeks of age), it's possible that she may not have been taught this lesson at all.

Either way, though, biting a human is unacceptable canine behavior. Every puppy needs to be taught that her teeth should never, ever contact human skin. Failure to learn this lesson will cause any pup to flunk Socialization 101—and could lead to big problems later in the dog's life. Dog bites are a leading cause of emergency room visits by humans, particularly children. The person whose canine companion puts too many teeth into her dealings with people runs a substantial risk of not only losing the dog but also of losing a lawsuit.

To nip a biting problem in the bud, it's crucial for you to teach your toothy tyke that making like a canine vampire is never, ever okay. The most effective way to do this is to make like a hurt littermate if your puppy's teeth come in contact with your person. In other words, if your puppy nips you, respond by yelping like a pup—and then move away.

In addition, a nipping incident should mean an immediate end to the activity that caused the nip to occur. And if that activity was a game in which you encouraged your puppy to play with and pounce on your hands or feet, think twice about playing that game in the future. It's unfair to correct your pup for biting when you were, essentially, goading her to do so.

Once you've made it clear that human flesh is not for chewing, take another minute to give your dog something that is okay for her to gnaw on, such as a chew toy. If she does start chewing on the toy, praise her and tell her what a good girl she is.

DOG PARK PROS AND CONS

Our community has just opened its first dog park, and I'm wondering whether it would be a good place to socialize my new dog.

A dog park can be a very good place to get your dog used to hanging out with other canines and their people.

Or, it can be very bad.

The great thing about dog parks is that they give your canine companion a chance to be with some of his own kind. Experts agree that time spent with other dogs can be great exercise and stimulation for any pooch. Moreover, many of the human companions of regular dog park visitors get to chat with each other while their dogs are frolicking—and those chats not only can lead to great friendships but also good information about dog care. As parents of human children can attest, there's nothing like the friendly ear and good advice of another mom or dad to help a beleaguered parent through the trials and tribulations that go with nurturing a dependent little being.

That said, a dog park might have a downside, too. You may not know all the dogs who habituate the park—particularly whether they've been fully immunized and whether their temperaments are suited for frolicking with other canines. As a matter of fact, your dog's temperament may be unsuited for such frolicking. Aggressive dogs, overly timid dogs, and (sometimes) relatively small dogs are not good candidates for the mixing-it-up that goes on at these canine gathering places.

To maximize the pros and minimize the cons of going to the dog park, try the following:

Know your dog. If your pooch is easily spooked, shows aggressiveness to any other dog, or is very small, going to a dog park may not be a good idea.

Know the other dogs. Try going to the dog park on your own a couple of times and surveying the regulars. If any of those habitual visitors appear unsuited for playing with other canines, think twice about going to that particular park.

Stay current on shots. Don't count on other doggie dog park denizens being protected against communicable diseases. Protect your own canine companion by making sure that he's current on all his immunizations.

Don't be aloof. If you do go to the park, let your dog get to know the other pooches there, while you chat up the humans who accompany those dogs. You'll probably make at least a few new friends with whom you may have more in common than many of the people you already know.

IF YOUR POOCH HATES THE DOG PARK

I tried taking my new dog to our local dog park, but he didn't seem to like it. All he did was bark at me for attention; he wasn't interested in the other dogs (even though they seemed interested in him). Does a dog have to go to a dog park to be properly socialized?

Taking your pooch to a dog park can be a terrific, no-hassle way to introduce him to other local canines—if he's comfortable with this kind of canine socializing. Unfortunately, some dogs don't like other dogs much. My own dog, Cory, is one of them. As a Sheltie, he's a relatively small dog; consequently, he seems pretty intimidated by some of the bigger dogs who tend to frequent such places.

Nevertheless, Cory gets plenty of opportunities to socialize with humans and canines alike. We often have people come over to our house, and we set up one-on-one play dates for him with other dogs who are his size or smaller. We also take him for car rides often, and for occasional trips to the pet store (although he doesn't like the sliding glass doors). He enjoys going for long walks around the neighborhood and meeting his favorite people—especially the mailman, who invariably gives him a treat.

The bottom line here: Dog parks are nice, but not mandatory. If your dog's not comfortable at one, don't force the issue.

SETTING UP PLAY DATES

Is setting up play dates for dogs a good idea? Do dogs really need to be with other dogs?

I suspect that if my own dog, Cory, could talk, he'd tell you that play dates for pooches are definitely a good idea. Cory's been having regular play dates with another Shetland sheepdog ever since both dogs were puppies. They like to nap together and, occasionally, chase each other around the house.

Regular play dates can benefit dogs in many ways. They can prevent a dog from becoming too dependent on her human companion; such dependence can lead to separation anxiety when the dog is left alone. In addition, these regular get-togethers can boost the confidence of a timid dog and help the very independent pooch learn to get along better with both dogs and people. And for many people, play dates between dogs allow them to have more control over who their dog interacts with than would be the case at a dog park.

To find a playmate for your pooch, scout around your neighborhood—either with or without your dog—to see if there are any other dogs who are hankering for canine company. Another way to find a friend for your Fido is to ask your vet whether she knows of any nearby dogs who are looking for another pooch to hang out with.

Then, once you find a possible playmate, make sure both dogs are compatible. Have them meet on neutral turf, such as a playground or park, instead of at the home of one or the other. Neither dog should show aggressiveness toward the other. Check, too, to see that the dogs seem to enjoy each other's company; many dogs have very clear preferences as to what kinds of dogs they like and don't like.

After that, let the dogs enjoy themselves—and each other.

TAKING A DOG TO WORK

I hate the idea of leaving my dog alone all day, and, fortunately, my company allows employees to bring their dogs to work. What do I need to do to make sure my dog will be a welcome guest at my company?

Kudos to your company for opening up its premises to pooches—and kudos to you for wanting your dog to be a good corporate citizen. Your bosses sound as though they're convinced of the results of a recent American Pet Product Manufacturers Association study that shows a drop in employee absenteeism when pets start making regular visits to an office. And you apparently realize that nothing shuts the corporate doors to office pets more quickly than one pet who misbehaves.

Experts suggest taking the following steps to ensure that everyone enjoys your dog's visits to your office:

Analyze your dog. Make sure your canine companion is really able to share your day at the office. Is he a quiet dog—or does he at least stop barking when told to? Is he friendly but calm when he meets people? And (perhaps most important of all) is he housetrained?

Analyze your coworkers. Even if your company officially welcomes dogs through its doors, your immediate coworkers may be less than thrilled about having a pooch in their midst. Make sure that no one who's likely to come in contact with your four-legged friend is allergic to dogs or afraid of them.

Prep your pooch. A good office dog is a well-trained dog. Make sure your dog consistently comes when called, knows how to sit and lie down when told, stops barking when ordered to do so, and knows not to jump up on people. Equally important is his bathroom reliability; if your dog has more than one accident, he may be *canis non grata* at your company. If your canine companion isn't up to speed on these and other basics of canine good manners, check out chapters fourteen and fifteen.

Bring the right stuff. To maximize your dog's comfort while in the hallowed halls of corporate America, it's important to bring along the right gear from home. This equipment includes a leash, up-to-date ID tags, a dog bed, non-messy treats that people can give your pooch, a few toys, and poop bags for cleaning up when taking doggie bathroom breaks.

Keep an eye on your friend. Make sure that your dog is truly happy hanging out in the office with you. If he starts to get cranky or unhappy at staying in a cubicle with you all day, rethink your policy of bringing him to your office. A part-time schedule may be better for him than being in the office full time.

RAISING A PARTY ANIMAL

We do a lot of entertaining at home, and I want to include my dog in our parties. Can I do that, or must he spend the evening in isolation?

The answer to that question depends on your dog's temperament, particularly his tolerance for large social gatherings. Some dogs love to hang out with large bunches of humans. I once attended a reception held by then-vice president Al Gore and Tipper Gore at the vice presidential residence—and while my husband and I were making our way to the receiving line, we saw the Gores' dog, a dignified black Labrador retriever, circulating with great aplomb among the guests who'd already shaken the Second Couple's hands. The crowd didn't appear to faze this dog in the least. He was mellow and responded calmly to all the friendly strangers' hands that reached out to pet him.

Other dogs, however, might not have the temperament to be such poised party animals. My own Sheltie, Cory, undoubtedly would spend much of the evening barking at our guests and trying to herd them into the center of the room! That said, he does fine when my husband and I have just a couple of people over for dinner. If we have a crowd, though, we usually put him in his crate so that he feels free to go off duty and sleep while we party.

If you're trying to decide whether your dog should help you host your next shindig, consider the following:

Is your dog mellow enough? If your canine companion is a laid-back, nothing-fazes-me type of pooch who enjoys meeting and greeting people, he might enjoy being a canine cohost. On the other hand, if your dog is very excitable, or is wary around new people, he probably should be left in peace—preferably in his beloved crate, or somewhere in the house that's away from the party action.

Is your house secure? Even if your dog is an ideal party animal, think twice about letting him mingle while your guests are arriving and leaving. In the chaos of party comings and goings, it's all too easy for your canine companion to slip out the door unnoticed.

Are there children among the guests? Although your own children probably know how to behave with dogs, other children may not. The result could be harassment for your dog or a child who gets bitten. Don't let your dog interact with kids outside your family unless you can supervise their interaction.

Is your dog a beggar? If your dog's primary purpose in partying is to score some unauthorized treats, it's a good idea to alert your guests beforehand. Too many treats can wreak havoc on a dog's tender tummy—and cleaning up the results of doggie indigestion is generally not conducive to happy partying.

A SOCIAL LIFE FOR THE HOME-ALONE DOG

The dog who spends most of her days home alone while her people are at school, work, or elsewhere needs extra help to develop the social life that every pooch is entitled to. Here are some ideas for filling up your home-alone dog's social calendar:

Get her out and about. Taking your four-legged friend for walks where people and pets abound can give her the social stimulation she needs and—if you walk long enough and briskly enough—can give you both a decent physical workout. A twenty-minute walk at least once a day, but preferably twice, will give your dog a stimulating taste of the world around her and will help her to deal with solitude better. If your excursions include regular visits to a dog park, so much the better.

Hire a dog walker. Most major metropolitan areas are chock-full of dog walkers—either individuals or companies—that will visit your home at midday and take your little darling for a good half-hour walk. Even better is when the dog walker is working with more than one pooch at a time. To find someone to take your dog for noontime walks, ask your vet or another dog owner for ideas and check out the classifieds of your local newspaper.

Set up regular play dates. Many home-alone dogs are much happier if they get to spend even one day a week with another dog and his at-home human companion. Check out your neighborhood and among your friends to see if such an arrangement is possible for your four-legged friend.

Opt for day care. Many major metro areas abound in doggie day care facilities that provide plenty of socialization opportunities for the home-alone dog. Check your Yellow Pages or search the Internet. While doggie day care can be a little pricey—in some areas they cost up to $130 per week per dog—such services may pay for themselves by saving you the cost of repairing or replacing furniture, carpets, and other household items that your otherwise lonesome pooch might chew to relieve stress or boredom.

Bring her to work. Check and see if your company might allow you to bring your four-legged friend to work with you one or two days a week. Many companies—particularly newer, more casual firms—don't mind if their employees bring their well-behaved pets to the office or job site occasionally. Your firm's human resources department can provide you with the information you need.

Try telecommuting. Working from home can give you some extra time with your canine companion and help assuage some of her loneliness. Depending on the type of job you have and your company's policies, you may be able to work from your home one or more days per week. Check with your supervisor and HR department to see if this option might work for you. (And of course, if you are self-employed, you can set your own dog-in-the-workplace policy). One caveat, though: Even though you're home, your dog needs to do more than lounge around in your office. Take time during the day for play breaks with her and schedule a midday walk in which you both can encounter other people and pets.

CHAPTER 13

Teaching Your New Dog

YOU CAN BE the best teacher your dog will ever have—if you're willing to tailor your teaching to the ways that your dog learns. To do that, you need to know a little bit about what makes your dog's brain tick. You also need to be committed to teaching him in the first place.

Surprisingly, a lot of people don't want to teach or train their dogs to do anything. The more honest among these folks say that they simply don't have the time to do the job. The more disingenuous nonteachers tend to claim that training a dog is unfair, or unnatural, or even manipulative. Nothing, however, could be further from the truth.

The fact is, dog training—when it's done right—is really just a matter of guiding the natural impulses and instincts your dog already has. For example, housetraining simply capitalizes on a dog's instinctive desire to refrain from pooping or peeing in the place where he eats and sleeps. Similarly, teaching a dog to sit just takes advantage of a dog's automatic impulse to train his eyes on a treat that you hold in your hand. In other words, training can be a win-win proposition for you and your four-legged friend. That proposition: By doing something that you want, your dog also gets something that he wants.

What are some of those canine desires? Here are just a few that, if you take advantage of them, can help you teach your dog what you want him to learn:

A place in the pack. If dogs had to choose between being alone and being with other individuals, they'd invariably choose the latter. That's because their ancient ancestors—like their wild cousins of today, the wolves—worked and played together in packs. Staying with the pack helped ensure each individual's survival.

Today, of course, most dogs have their basic needs taken care of; consequently, they don't need to be in a pack to survive physically. But they still have a great emotional need to belong to a pack, be it human, canine, or both. Your dog's intense desire to belong to your pack—even if the pack consists of just you and him—is an instinct that you can tap in order to accelerate his learning curve.

A leader to please. Belonging to a pack helps fulfill a deep-seated emotional need within your canine companion—but for optimal learning, he also needs to know exactly what his rank in that pack is. And if you want to be his teacher, his rank should be subordinate, while yours needs to be one of leadership—the top dog, if you will.

In asserting this leadership, you don't have to imitate the alpha wolves you see on PBS or Animal Planet documentaries. There's no need for you to growl, employ a death-ray stare, or roll your dog onto his back in order to demonstrate your top-of-the-pack ranking. You simply need to be the individual who sets the agenda and makes all the decisions with respect to your dog's care and welfare. You need to be a benevolent leader whom your dog will do just about anything to please.

A den of his own. Wolf packs generally like to live in small, dark places that are at least partially enclosed on three sides, but have an opening through which the pack members can peer out into the world without the world peering back at them. This place is called a den—and, like so many other ancient canine instincts, the desire for a den lives on in domestic dogs.

Of course, domestic dogs don't have caves within which to hide from the world. But the houses in which they live offer plenty of other potential dens. My own dog, Cory, likes to hide under my desk while I'm working. But his favorite den is the one we've provided for him: his crate.

The crate doesn't just offer Cory and other canines a place in which to feel safe and secure. It's also—as you'll see in chapter fourteen—an indispensable housetraining tool. That's because dogs will do just about anything to avoid eliminating in or otherwise soiling their dens. Consequently, you can use your dog's attachment to his den to develop his capacity for controlling his urges to poop and pee until you want him to.

A predictable life. Unlike their human companions, dogs do not get bored by doing the same thing at the same time every day. In fact, they thrive on such consistency and predictability. Knowing what's going to happen—and when it will happen—seems to jump-start a dog's intelligence, not to mention his bodily instincts. For example, if you feed him and take him for a walk at the same times every day, he'll soon train his body to eliminate at those times. And if you say the same phrase to him every time he eliminates, he may actually learn to associate that phrase with the performance of potty maneuvers—so that you can actually command him to do his bathroom business and count on him to comply.

These are just a few of the basic doggie desires that you can influence to your advantage. However, the way you exert your influence is crucial. In other words, your training style will determine whether your dog is a happy student or a reluctant learner.

Most dogs of a generation ago probably were reluctant learners. Why? Because we humans didn't know how to make training a win-win enterprise. We would "housebreak" a dog to teach him basic bathroom manners. We'd forcibly push a dog's tush to the floor to make him sit. And, most notoriously, we'd yank our dogs around on so-called choke chains to teach them to walk nicely with us.

Fortunately, those days are passing. Today, we use incentives such as treats, hugs, and verbal praise to coax dogs and other animals into learning what we're trying to teach them. Instead of punishing them for doing something wrong, we reward them for doing something right. This new, gentler form of training is called "positive reinforcement"—and you'll see many examples of how to use positive reinforcement techniques in chapters fourteen and fifteen.

Positive reinforcement rewards the dog for doing what you want him to do.

WHEN TO START TRAINING

I've heard that you shouldn't start training a puppy until she's six months old. But that seems to give a pup an awful lot of time to pick up some bad habits. Do I really need to wait until she's six months old before I start teaching her anything, or taking her to an obedience class?

You're absolutely right to be skeptical about the old no-training-till-six-months rule. Waiting that long gives the dog way too much time to teach herself what you don't want her to learn. Such a postponement also wastes a puppy's innate intelligence and eagerness to bond with the person who's raising her.

Gentle, introductory training can begin as soon as you bring your little one home. In fact, rudimentary housetraining, as you'll see in chapter fourteen, can begin as soon as you leave the breeder's. Other lessons, such as learning to walk on a leash, coming when called, and sitting on command also can begin in early puppyhood, as part of your effort to socialize your little darling. Just keep the lessons, which are explained in chapter fifteen, short enough to accommodate a puppy's limited attention span.

You also don't have to wait till the half-year mark to enroll your puppy in formal classes. Plenty of communities offer "puppy kindergarten" classes for dogs who are four months of age or even younger. Just make sure to ask the instructor whether every canine student will be checked for immunizations—and make sure the instructor herself eschews coercive devices like choke collars. For all dogs, but especially puppies, positive training is much more effective than forcible, correction-based training.

TO TREAT OR NOT TO TREAT

I don't like the idea of using treats to train my dog; it feels as though I'm bribing him. Shouldn't it be enough for him to get my praise?

Eventually, your dog will probably do what you want him to just to hear the sound of your beloved voice. But when you're trying to teach him something new, a more concrete incentive, such as a tasty treat, will accelerate his learning curve.

Sometimes a little benign bribery—like flattery—can really get you somewhere with whomever you're interacting with. That's particularly true with a dog, who doesn't have the benefit of being able to speak or even understand much of the English language. A carefully timed treat cuts across the human–canine language barrier. That proffered goodie shows your dog that if he does what you ask, he'll get that drool-inducing reward he's longing for. And sometimes, as you'll see in chapter fifteen, the treat can actually direct the dog to do what you want him to.

Once your dog learns whatever maneuver you're teaching him, though, you can start tapering off the treats. Use them occasionally to remind him that good things come to pooches who obey—or more consistently if you're asking him to do something that's difficult to do. For example, I always offer Cory a treat when I ask him to lie down and refrain from barking when my husband leaves for work in the morning (a situation that invariably provokes frenzied barking from Cory unless I intervene). Complying with that request is very difficult for Cory, but when he sees me get out the treat bag, that compliance seems to get at least a little bit easier.

USING A CLICKER

I hear a lot about a technique called clicker training. What exactly is it?

Clicker training is a technique that makes positive reinforcement training especially effective. When your dog does something that you want him to do, you use a toy clicker—a small box with a metal strip that makes a clicking sound when it's pushed and then released—to tell him that he's done the right thing. Immediately after using the clicker, you give the dog a treat.

The clicker provides a clear, unmistakable, immediate signal to your dog that he's done something right and that something good is going to happen. He soon learns to repeat that action in order to hear the click and get the treat. Scientists call this kind of training operant conditioning.

But whatever you call it—clicker training or operant conditioning—this technique works very well, particularly with dogs who have proven stubborn or difficult to train. And dogs aren't the only animals who learn to love the clicker. Dolphins, cats, horses, and even human beings have learned the power of positive training through their trainers' use of the clicker.

THE EXTRA-PERCEPTIVE POOCH

I've heard about dogs who know when a person is going to have an epileptic seizure, or who can detect skin cancer, or who somehow just know when something is going to happen. How can that be? Do dogs have ESP?

The possibility that dogs and other animals have a "sixth sense" has tantalized human beings for a long time. But in many cases, that apparent sixth sense is really just an amplification of one of the more familiar five: the sense of smell. The dog's nose has more than forty times the number of cells that a human nose has. That makes the canine sniffer capable of detecting odors that are way beyond the capacity of its human counterpart.

For example, experiments in Florida with a retired police dog appeared to indicate that malignant melanomas emit a distinctive odor that the dog could be trained to detect. Similarly, scientists have speculated that epileptics emit certain odors before they have a seizure—

and that the dog picks up on that change in scent. Either way, though, the dog's sensing ability is no less wondrous for being rooted in the same sense of smell that so many animals (including the human animal) possess.

In other cases, though, the dog's highly developed powers of observation are what cues him to an impending event. My husband and I have often marveled at the ability of Cory, our Sheltie, to know when we are about to serve dinner—no matter when we do so or what we do beforehand. We haven't figured out exactly how we tip him off to the impending start of supper—but we realize, just by seeing how intently he studies us, that he could easily pick up on cues that we don't even know we're giving.

In other words, dogs probably don't have a sixth sense—but what they do with the five senses they do have can be pretty amazing.

DOES SIZE MATTER?

I am a very small woman—and my kids, obviously, are smaller than I am. We don't look like leaders of any pack. How can any of us convey leadership to the full-grown Lab we just adopted?

To your new Labrador retriever, being an effective leader has nothing to do with his size, or your relative lack thereof. I can attest personally to the utter irrelevance of size to successful dog training. I'm only five foot two, and weigh barely 100 pounds. But Cory, my Sheltie, and any other dog I've ever lived with was happy to accept my leadership—even when I was a kid (and smaller than I am now). No matter what your age or size, your dog will look to you for leadership if you act like a leader.

That means that you need to be the one who decides when the dog is fed, when the dog gets playtime, and when the dog goes for a walk. It means you don't put up with having your leashed canine pull you down the street as though you're both in training for the Iditarod. And it certainly means that you set clear, consistent expectations for your dog—and do so in ways that he can understand.

Which brings us to tone of voice.

Your tone of voice can convey multiple meanings to your dog, even though he probably understands no more than one or two dozen words of English. That's because you can vary the pitch at which you speak to your canine companion. For example, a firm, decisive tone of voice will get your dog's attention when you want him to do something specific, such as sit or lie down. A soft, high-pitched voice will make it clear that you're happy with what your pooch has done. And a stern, low-pitched voice will sound unmistakably like a growl of disapproval to your eager-to-please pup.

Moreover, any person of any size can take on these tones of voice. Some are more challenging than others: For example, a child might be better at giving praise than giving a command. A deep-voiced man might experience exactly the opposite difficulty. But it's worth the effort to keep trying—and your dog can help. That's because, if you're consistent in the tones of voice you use to convey various messages, your dog will soon pick up on what you're trying to say.

DO DOGS FEEL GUILTY?

Picture this: You're headed home after a long hard day of battling office politicians and beating impossible deadlines. Understandably, you're looking forward to a friendly greeting from your beloved dog, a relaxing walk with him around the block to calm your frazzled nerves, and a low-key evening watching the tube, with him nearby to pet and cuddle.

Then you enter your home—and nearly step in a stinky little puddle, which is next to an equally putrid little pile. And next to both smelly little presents is your dog, who has taken one look at you and started cringing.

As you stomp through the house to get a paper towel and dog doo cleaner, your dog's tail droops between his back legs. And when you turn to glare at him, he looks away from you, as though he's afraid to meet your eyes.

Most people would say that your cringing canine knows that he's messed up—literally—and is exhibiting his guilt over having done so. But those people would be wrong.

Although dogs are incredibly sensitive beings, guilt and remorse are not in their emotional lexicons. Your fearful Fido is reacting to you, not to his misdeed. In fact, he doesn't even know that he's done anything wrong. He only perceives, thanks to the change in your body language, that you're angry. And if you yell at him and say his name, he'll realize very quickly that you are angry at him.

But he still won't know why. He won't connect your anger with the two malodorous presents that greeted your arrival. In fact, he's forgotten about those presents altogether. He created them too long ago—like, five whole minutes ago—for him to remember those creative acts. His cringing and cowering don't mean that he feels bad about what he's done. He's simply a scared pooch—and you're the one who's scaring him.

Dogs just can't connect the anger you exhibit with an act they performed even a few minutes ago. Consequently, even yelling at your dog—much less hitting him or otherwise punishing him—will teach him nothing except to be afraid of you. And fear has no place in *any* teacher-student relationship. The bottom line here is that if your dog screws up, you probably have screwed up. Realize that there's nothing you can do about the current mistake, but you can make sure that you (and he) don't make similar mistakes in the future.

CHAPTER 14

Housetraining Your New Dog

F EW THINGS TUG at the human heart more than a row of dogs at an animal shelter. Each of these pooches has lost at least one home; each is hoping to find a new place to live and a new person to love. And, in most cases, each faces a high-stakes deadline: the need to find that new home and new person by a particular date—or face euthanasia.

What brings these former pets to this critical juncture? All too often, it's because they haven't learned proper bathroom behavior. In other words, they've failed to master the not-so-difficult art of being housetrained.

The pooch who fails to potty properly misses out on a lot of the good things in a dog's life. Even if he doesn't draw a one-way ticket to the local animal shelter, his life isn't nearly as good as it could be. That's because the unpottied pooch often finds himself spending time alone in a basement, garage, or a backyard. There, his people reason, the dog's unwelcome puddles or piles won't cause permanent damage like they could in a nicely carpeted living room or family room.

Certainly, exiling the dog who flunks basic housetraining can prevent carpets and floors from suffering permanent damage; however, the damage this does to the dog—not to mention to the bond with his human companion—can be considerable. That's because the dog is an intensely social animal. He loves nothing more than to hang out with his pack, be it human or canine. Being relegated to a room away from the social action is agony for most dogs.

The people who create that social action lose out, too. After all, most of us welcome dogs into our households in order to experience the special joys of canine companionship. When a pooch's potty problems force us to send him into social exile, we don't experience that companionship.

What's saddest about such states of affairs is that they're totally unnecessary. Any dog can be housetrained, if the humans in his life are willing to spend some time undertaking that training. Those humans need just a little time, a little patience, the willingness to be consistent, and an understanding of some basic canine instincts.

But just what is housetraining? On the surface, the answer to that question is simple: A housetrained dog is a dog who does his bath-

Teach your dog to potty where and when you want him to.

Table 14.1 Indoors or Out?

Method	Pros	Cons
Indoor	No need to walk outside No need for fence Dog can potty anytime	Can be messy Can be stinky Need to bring paper, litter while traveling
Outdoor	No dog messes in the house Easier traveling	Dog must be walked or fenced Dog can eliminate only at certain times

room business only where and when the humans in his life want him to do it. Scratch the surface, though, and the answer becomes a little bit more complicated, simply because different humans have different lifestyles—and different priorities.

Some humans, such as those who live in a high-rise apartment or who have difficulty getting around, might want their pooches to potty indoors. The indoor canine bathroom can come in one of three forms: newspapers spread out on the floor, a doggie litter box, or puppy training pads that are spread on the floor like a sheet of newspaper.

Other people, however, can't stand the thought of using any parts of their houses as canine bathrooms. Those people will choose to restrict their pooches' pit stops to outdoor locations. The canine outhouse can either be a designated spot in your own backyard, or places where your Bowser does his business while you walk him.

But no matter where you choose to place your dog's bathroom, the theory behind successful housetraining is the same: Instead of catching your dog having a bathroom accident, you prevent your dog from having those accidents in the first place. Sound impossible? It's not— if you're willing to capitalize on your dog's instinctive desire to never, ever soil his den.

Before dogs chose to live with people, they lived together in packs —and each pack lived in a dark, snug, cavernous little place called a den. Almost from infancy, the puppies in these dens learned an important rule of the house: to potty away from the den. Cleanliness wasn't the only issue here, though; by leaving their stinky bathroom deposits some distance from the den, the pups could deflect predators from the den.

Today, of course, domestic dogs generally don't need to worry about predators. But a dog's desire to live in a clean den—which, for the typical twenty-first century pooch, is a crate—gives the savvy human a big advantage in housetraining. That's because whenever you can't watch your canine housetrainee to make sure he doesn't have an accident, you can put him in his crate, where he will do his darndest to keep himself from having that accident.

Here is a step-by-step guide to easy, effective housetraining:

Step One: Pick a potty spot. If you're training your puppy or dog to potty outdoors, choose a grassy area that's close to your home and easy to clean up. The indoor canine housetrainee needs to have a litter box, sheets of newspaper, or potty pads in an uncarpeted area that's away from household traffic. Whether indoors or out, take your canine companion to this spot whenever he needs to go—and, if possible, use the same route to get there every time you take him.

Step Two: Supervise your pup. The key to effective housetraining is to prevent accidents from occurring in the first place. To make sure your pooch is accident-free, watch him closely any time he's not confined. That way, when you see the pup showing signs of needing to go (stopping suddenly, circling, and/or sniffing the floor), you can whisk him to the potty spot before he actually does the deed.

Step Three: Get him a den. When you can't watch your housetrainee, put him in his crate. That way, your dog's keep-the-den-clean reflex will kick in, and you can go about your business knowing that your dog probably won't want to do his.

There's one caveat to the den rule: Don't leave your dog in the crate for too long—certainly no more than three or four hours. Puppies should stay in crates even less time: never for any more hours than their ages in months (for example, a maximum of two hours for a two-month-old animal).

Step Four: Schedule bathroom breaks. Most dogs like to eliminate after eating and before bedtime. Puppies need more frequent pit stops: after sleeping, eating, and playing, and before bedtime. By setting up a schedule for those activities, you can make your canine housetrainee's bathroom breaks more predictable and thus reduce his chances of having an accident.

Here's a typical schedule for a three-month-old puppy:

6:30 A.M.: Take your puppy out of the crate, attach the leash, and go together to the indoor or outdoor potty spot. Stay quiet as the puppy sniffs, paces, or circles. When she starts to poop or pee, praise her quietly. Once she's done, give her a small treat and more praise; then play with her for a few minutes.

7:00 A.M.: Come inside and give your puppy some breakfast. Fifteen to twenty minutes later, take her to the potty spot and follow the 6:30 A.M. routine. When she's done, take her inside and put her in her crate.

Mid-morning: Take your puppy out of her crate and to her potty spot. Follow the potty routine, then put her back into her crate. (If your dog's over four months old, you can skip this break.)

12:00 noon: Take your pup to the potty place, follow the potty routine, then come inside. Feed her some lunch, spend some time playing, then take her back to her potty place. (If your dog's over four months old, you can skip lunch.) After you're both done, put your pup in the crate.

Mid-afternoon: Same as mid-morning. (You can skip this if your dog's past the four-month mark.)

5:00 P.M.: Take your pooch to her potty spot, follow the potty routine, then come inside. Feed dinner, then take her back to the potty spot for another round of the potty routine. Once your dog has mastered housetraining, she won't need the post-dinner pit stop.

Evening: Play with your canine companion as much as possible, but watch her very closely. She'll need to take bathroom breaks much more frequently now, when she's active, than during the day, when she was quieter.

10:00 to 11:00 P.M.: Take your four-legged friend to her potty spot for one last rendering of the potty routine. Then, put her in her crate for the night. Unless your dog is under twelve weeks of age, she should be able to sleep through the night without a bathroom break.

During the night: Puppies younger than twelve weeks of age will probably need to empty their bladders some time during the night. If you hear your canine baby whining or acting restless, get out of bed, take her out, and follow the potty routine. Then, put the pup in the crate for the rest of the night.

Step Five: Stay with it. It'll take some time for your pooch to become a housetraining graduate. Most pups don't have the physical control they need to be completely reliable until they're about six months old. Adult dogs have the control, but still may need time to figure out what your potty protocol is. Either way, don't consider your pooch completely housetrained until she's been accident-free for at least a month.

WHY A SCHEDULE?

Why is it important to have a schedule when housetraining a puppy or dog? I don't go to the bathroom according to any set timetable; why do I need one for my pooch?

Adopting a consistent routine for your housetrainee's eating and eliminating helps your dog become housetrained much faster than if you take a "whatever, whenever" approach. That's because dogs learn through repetition. If you have him eating, drinking, peeing, and pooping at the same times and places each and every day, he'll soon expect to be doing all those things at the times and places you've decided. And that expectation will be both mental and physical. Mentally, he'll soon anticipate that it's time to venture outside or over to the newspapers. Physically, his body will anticipate the same thing. In short, by keeping to a schedule, you help his housetraining become a habit.

Once your dog becomes a reliable housetraining graduate, you won't need to be so rigid in scheduling his bathroom breaks. That's because your canine genius will have the physical control he needs to hold his fire a few more minutes if your schedule changes unexpectedly. Still, in the long run, it's better for you and for your four-legged friend to keep at least the framework of a routine for bathroom and dining activities.

HOLDING TIME

How long can a dog hold his urine?

That depends on the dog. My own dog, Cory, has a personal best of nearly twenty-four hours—and not because he didn't have a chance to open his floodgates sooner. He just didn't like the conditions (rainy, chilly) in which he had to do the deed. But experts don't recommend testing to see if your dog's bladder is made of iron. They recommend limiting an adult dog's holding time to no more than eight to ten hours.

If your dog fails to urinate for any reason when trying to do so, don't wait for ten hours to see if he produces some pee. Get him to the vet as soon as possible so that he can be tested for a possible obstruction in his urinary tract.

AN INDOOR/OUTDOOR DOG?

Most of the time I want to take my dog outside to do her business, but every now and then (like on a rainy night or when I want to sleep in on the weekends) I'd like to be able to spread a couple of newspapers on the floor for her to use indoors. Is this possible?

I wouldn't advise trying to teach your dog to be an indoor/outdoor pottyer. Any effort to do so is likely to only cause confusion in your canine's mind. The result of such confusion, alas, is likely to be multiple puddles and piles in all the wrong places, not to mention a dog who doesn't know what to do when taken to either her indoor or outdoor potty spot.

Rest assured that when your dog reaches adulthood, she'll be able to hold her water long enough for you to get a few extra z's on weekend mornings. As for going outdoors in bad weather, your best bet is to be sure your pooch needs to potty before taking her out in rain or snow. If she needs to go, you can count on her doing so, no matter what the weather is.

There is, of course, one situation where you'll need to let your dog potty both indoors and out: when you're gone all day but live with a puppy who requires a noontime bathroom break. If this describes your dog and your life, you'll need to spread out some newspapers for your little one during the day until he develops enough control to stay dry all day. More about how to juggle this special situation appears in the next question.

WHAT IF I WORK ALL DAY?

I have a four-month-old puppy who needs to be housetrained—but I work outside my home all day. Does he really need a noontime break?

In a word: Yes. A four-month-old puppy can't be expected to hold his water for more than four hours. For that reason, a midday potty break of some sort is essential to his comfort and urinary tract health—not to mention his prospects for becoming housetrained.

Ideally, you or someone else should visit your four-legged friend around noon each workday to potty him and play with him. The latter activity is almost as important as the potty part. That's because puppies are intensely social little beings, and they crave contact with other individuals. If you can be that individual, so much the better: Perhaps your office is close enough to your home to allow you to do noontime bathroom duty. And if your company is especially laid back (or if you're the company owner!), you may even be able to bring your puppy to work with you.

If you can't provide your puppy with noontime relief yourself, you may be able to find someone who can, such as a dog-loving neighbor, or a professional dog walker. For the latter, check with your vet to see whether there are any dog-walking or pet-sitting services in your area.

What if you strike out on your effort to find a noontime visitor for your canine companion? Unfortunately, you'll need to create an indoor potty for your pup to use during the day. Confine your four-legged friend to your kitchen or other easily cleaned area with baby gates or an ex-pen and spread several layers of newspapers on the floor. Let your dog perform *only* his midday whiz and deposit on these papers; take him outside the rest of the time. In another couple of months—or when the papers are unused for at least a week—you can declare victory and put away the papers forevermore.

DEALING WITH ACCIDENTS

I know that the whole idea behind housetraining is to keep accidents from happening in the first place—but, hey, nobody's perfect! What should I do if my dog makes a mistake?

Here's what you *don't* do: make a big deal of the "mistake." Simply clean up the toileting transgression without comment. Use an enzymatic cleaner designed specifically for cleaning up pet accidents: Three good ones are Nature's Miracle, Simple Solutions, and Anti-Icky-Poo.

Then, ask yourself what you could have done to prevent the accident. Did you wait too long between bathroom breaks? Did you take your eyes off your four-legged friend just long enough for him to sneak off and make an unauthorized deposit? Did you (gulp!) forget one of his scheduled bathroom breaks? Be honest with yourself, and you're likely to discover why your pooch pooped or peed where he wasn't supposed to. Then, resolve to not make the same mistake again.

CLEANING UP OUTSIDE

Our town requires us to pick up after our dogs when we walk them. Exactly how do I do that?

Your town is hardly alone. Across America and around the rest of the world, municipalities of all sizes are taking a tough stand on canine waste cleanup. Mayors and city councils now understand that, left untended, dog stool can add all kinds of toxic bacteria to a city's water supply. And while treatment plants can remove those contaminants, it's much cheaper for people to just clean up after their pets.

Cleaning up need not be a big production or even all that gross. All you need is an oblong plastic bag, such as the one your daily newspaper arrives in, or the bag that protects a loaf of bread. Once you have the bag in hand and the poop's hit the ground, here's what you do:

1. Pull the bag over one of your hands.
2. Pick up the poop with the hand that's got the bag over it.
3. Grasp the open end of the bag with your other hand, and pull the bag inside out.
4. Knot the bag (which now has the poop in it) and drop it into a trashcan.

WHEN A DOG WETS HER BED

My dog sometimes pees in her bed while she's asleep. What's going on?

Many older, spayed female dogs wet their beds while they sleep, but vets have what these dogs need to stay dry: a short course of diethylstilbestrol, which is also known as DES. This compound contains the same properties as natural estrogens, the loss of which contribute to a dowager doggie's bedwetting.

One strong caution, however: Pregnant women should never administer DES to their dogs. The reason: the compound can cause miscarriages, birth defects, and long-term problems to human babies.

PEEING IN THE CRATE

My puppy doesn't use his crate as a den; he uses it as his potty! How can I housetrain him?

Start off by getting a new crate—or at least a new crate mattress and bedding, so that there's no scent from your dog's previous mistakes to lure him into repeating his performance.

Then, check to see whether the crate you're using is too big for your canine companion. The crate should be just big enough for your dog to stand up and turn around; if it's any bigger, your dog will probably eliminate at one end of the crate and sleep at the other. You can construct the crate divider described in chapter four to make the crate small enough to be the snug, secure den it's supposed to be.

Another reason why your dog is using his crate as his toilet is because that's all he knows how to do. For example, dogs who are raised in the puppy mills I describe in chapter two often are forced to stay in their crates twenty-four hours a day, seven days a week. Eventually, their floodgates give way and they eliminate in their crates. Soon, they've lost the instinct to keep their dens clean; instead, they think that their dens are also their potties.

If crate size or your pooch's past isn't the problem, your crating policy may be. No dog can hold it forever—and if you leave your puppy in his crate for more than a couple of hours during the day, he won't be able to keep his floodgates shut. Make sure that your puppy isn't crated any longer than the number of hours equal to his months in age, for example, no more than three hours for a three-month-old pup.

HEEDING PRE-POTTY SIGNALS

How do I know when my dog is about to poop or pee? Sometimes my dog doesn't give me any signals at all; he just stops in the middle of whatever he's doing and goes. How can I anticipate him if he doesn't give me anything to anticipate?

Most dogs do give pretty clear signals that a bathroom anointing or deposit is imminent. Some walk around in circles; others pace back and forth. Many dogs start sniffing the ground intently. And some dogs—my own dog, Cory, is one of them—do all three.

Clearly, then, dogs are highly individualistic in their pre-potty routines. Their individuality in these and other areas of life makes it incumbent upon us, their human companions, to learn what our particular pooches do to signal us about what's coming. Some dogs, however, force us to refine our powers of observation to acutely sensitive levels. That's because such dogs' peeing (and pooping) cues are so subtle that they appear to be giving us no warning at all. This is especially true of young puppies, who often don't know that they're about to do their business until they actually start to do it.

If your dog is the subtle sort, you need to pay attention to other factors. Ask yourself the following questions:

When was his previous potty break? If it's been more than a couple of hours, he may need another pit stop—especially if he's a puppy.
What's he been doing? If your canine companion has just eaten, drunk some water, gotten up from a nap, or has been playing hard, he could probably use a trip to his potty spot.

Is something going to happen? If someone's coming over to visit you, or you're about to go out of the house for a little while, or the activity you and pooch have been involved in is about to change, a bathroom break is always a good idea.

As time passes, you'll get to know your dog better—and he'll get to know his own body better! Once you both acquire such knowledge, his I've-gotta-go signals may become a lot more obvious than they appear to be now.

POTTY PROBLEMS THAT AREN'T POTTY PROBLEMS

All too often, a dog who appears to have potty problems may actually be sick. That's why, whenever your dog has housetraining lapses, your first step should be to have his veterinarian check him out. Here are some potty problems that are actually signs that a dog could be sick:

Peeing all the time. The dog whose bladder appears to be working overtime may actually have a urinary tract infection (UTI). Such a dog needs a vet's attention and some antibiotics to clear up the infection. However, you can help relieve your dog's discomfort in the meantime by giving him more frequent bathroom breaks and encouraging him to drink lots of water.

Constant drinking and constant peeing. If the weather isn't abnormally hot, but your pooch suddenly starts drinking more water than usual and, consequently, pees more than usual, he needs to see a vet right away. Such symptoms may indicate that your dog has diabetes, kidney problems, or Cushing's disease (a condition that results when the adrenal glands produce too much cortisone).

Straining to pee. The dog who's clearly trying to urinate to little or no avail may be suffering from a life-threatening case of stones in the urinary tract. Prompt evaluation by a veterinarian is critical.

Weird-looking urine. A dog's urine is normally yellow. If your dog's pee is a darker color, such as rust or red, he's got blood in his urine, which results from either a UTI or an internal injury. Light-colored or clear urine—especially first thing in the morning, when urine is more likely to be highly concentrated and a strong yellow color—could mean that your dog's kidneys aren't retaining enough water. Such failure could indicate one of several diseases. Any way you look at it, a dog whose urine isn't the normal color needs prompt veterinary attention.

Diarrhea. Dogs get the runs fairly often, and much of the time it's not a big deal. To treat it at home, hold off on feeding your four-legged friend for twenty-four hours or so, to give his tummy time to calm down. Make sure he drinks plenty of water, though, to pre-vent the dehydration that can accompany diarrhea. Once the first twenty-four hours have passed, feed him a bland diet of boiled hamburger and rice. If he's still got diarrhea after a day on the bland diet, call your vet. Call sooner—as in right away—if your pooch is a puppy.

Constipation. Sometimes, pooches (like people) get a little anal retentive (so to speak). Some dietary adjustment can often do the trick if your dog gets constipated. Try giving him some vegetables, such as carrots, broccoli, green beans, or beets, with his meal; the fiber in those veggies may jump-start your canine's colon. Make sure, too, that he drinks plenty of water and gets sufficient exer-cise. If those measures don't do the trick in twenty-four hours, call your vet: Your dog could be suffering from a blockage somewhere in his digestive tract.

Weird-looking stool. A dog's stool should be firm, compact, and not make much of a stink. Deviations from that norm could mean trouble. Poop that's soft, stinky, and full of mucus could indicate the presence of Giardia, a parasite that dogs (or humans) pick up if they drink contaminated water. Gray, greasy stool accompanied by stubborn diarrhea may be a sign of pancreatic problems. Black poop may signal bleeding from the upper digestive tract, while blood streaks in the stool could mean irritation in colon or rectum. All of these conditions require a vet's attention.

CHAPTER 15

Building Your New Dog's Knowledge

PICTURE THIS: YOU'RE carrying a large object out of your house. To do so, you need to prop open your front door so that it doesn't smack you in the face on your way out. Alas, that open door creates a great doggie escape route—but your canine companion knows that she has to stay in the house, no matter what. And she does.

Think that keeping a dog from bolting through an open door is impossible? Think again. My own dog, Cory, has learned to be just about bolt-proof. That's because before I open our front door, I tell him to "stay"—which is the word he equates with not moving an inch away from where he currently is. In fact, I can't remember a single time Cory has failed to stay inside the door when told to do so.

That's just one example of how a dog who knows a few crucial commands is much easier to live with than an uneducated canine. And, of course, one of those crucial commands is to "stay" when told.

Teaching your new dog some basic commands doesn't have to be difficult. First, you need the right equipment: your slightly hungry

SEVEN TEMPTING TREATS FOR YOUR NEW DOG

- Microwaved hot dog bits
- Rice cakes
- Green beans
- Carrots
- Frozen broccoli florets
- Liver-flavored commercial treats
- Small apple slices

pooch; a generous supply of his favorite treats (microwaved bits of hot dog are Cory's particular favorite); and a six-foot leash.

Next, you need to take the right approach—in other words, you need to create the conditions in which your dog can best learn what you're trying to teach him. That means providing an environment that downplays distractions, such as the television, children horsing around, or lots of outdoor commotion, which can divert your dog's attention from learning his behavioral basics. Also important is keeping each session short: no more than five minutes for puppies under four months of age and a maximum of ten minutes for older pups and adult dogs. Most important of all is keeping the session sweet: Always end a lesson by asking your dog to do something he already knows how to do—and when he does, heap on the praise and give him a treat.

Now that you and your canine companion are prepped—both physically and mentally—for training, here's how to teach the basic commands every dog should know.

THE SIT

This command is just about the easiest maneuver that you can teach your four-legged friend. Here's what to do:

- Start by holding a treat in front of your dog's nose; make sure he's looking at the little goodie.
- Tell him, "Sit"—then, move the treat straight up till it's just over the dog's head. At that point, move the treat back toward his rear end.

- As your dog follows your hand with his eyes, he'll automatically sit down. When that happens, praise your pal and give him the treat.

THE DOWN

This maneuver follows the same principle as the sit—but make sure he knows the sit before teaching this command. Once your dog is sitting, do the following:

- Hold a treat in front of his face, and make sure he's looking at it.
- Say "Down," in a long, drawn-out tone so that you're really saying "Dooowwwwn."
- At the same time, move your hand down to the ground about six inches in front of your dog; then, move outward along the ground several more inches. (The effect should be that your hand moves in an L-shaped path.)
- As the dog follows your hand with his eyes, he'll lie down. When he does, praise him and give him the treat.

THE STAY

This command tells your dog to remain where he is. Although it's often paired with the sit or the down, the stay can also tell a dog to remain standing wherever he is—as I've discovered with Cory whenever I open our front door. Start by placing your dog in a sit or down. Then:

- Place your open palm about six inches from his nose.
- Say "Stay," in the same long, drawn-out tone that you use for the down.
- Move back one step, then return immediately.
- Praise your pooch for staying, and give him a treat.
- Repeat the process, moving back two steps this time. Gradually increase the distance you move away from your dog; then boost

the length of time he must stay. Finally, start working amid distractions in his environment. When your dog can hold his stay for a good five minutes, while you're at the other end of your house and other people come and go, you can consider the command taught!

Coming when called is one of the most important lessons your dog can learn.

THE RECALL

Also known as coming when called, this is probably the toughest—but most important—command you can teach your canine companion. Start by placing your friend in the sit position a few feet away from you. Then:

- Say your dog's name and the word *come* in a happy, enthusiastic tone of voice. Jump up and down happily if he doesn't start coming.
- As your dog comes to you, squat down and open your arms.
- When your dog reaches you, welcome him enthusiastically and give him a treat.

- Repeat the process, but gradually increase the distance between you. And even when your dog has mastered this maneuver, keep practicing it—but in a fun setting, such as hiding and calling him to come find you.

THE OFF

The "Off" command prompts a dog to reverse course, no matter what he's doing. If he's fishing through the wastebasket, a crisply spoken "Off" will get his nose out of the trash; if he's interested in the chicken bone someone left on the sidewalk, a sharply spoken "Off!" will keep him from making a dangerous attempt to eat it.

- Begin by placing your dog's favorite toy on the ground a few feet away from him. When he heads for the toy, pick it up and say "Off!" in a loud, commanding voice that will startle your dog.
- As he looks at you in surprise (he will), praise him in a high, sweet-sounding voice—and then give him the toy.
- Repeat until he instantly drops a toy when he hears the command. Practice this one often!

WALKING ON LEASH

Nothing makes a walk more pleasurable than being accompanied by a pooch who knows how to behave himself while he's on the leash— and nothing makes a walk more miserable than a canine walking companion who thinks the two of you are training for a dog-sled race. To ensure that your dog fits the former category, here's what to do:

- Leash your dog and place the leash loop around your wrist.
- Grasp the leash with the looped hand just below the loop. With the opposite hand, hold the leash about halfway down its length.
- Have your dog stand next to you on the side opposite your looped hand, so that the leash falls diagonally across your body.

- Tell your dog "Let's walk!" in a cheerful but decisive voice, and start walking briskly. As you walk, chat with your dog so that he pays attention to you.
- If he bolts out in front of you, let him go the full length of the leash. Then, turn around suddenly—but without jerking the leash—and walk in the opposite direction. Your surprised pooch will soon learn to pay attention to you instead of whatever's causing him to run ahead.
- When you stop, remove your unlooped hand from the leash and place it in front of your dog's face so that he stops, too.

The foregoing behavioral basics make up what every dog needs to know to be considered to have a modicum of manners. But if you don't want to stop there, the following are some other maneuvers you can teach your canine companion.

PEEING ON COMMAND

Wouldn't it be great to be able to take your dog outside late at night or in bad weather and have him pee as soon as you tell him to? Happily, a lot of pooches can learn just that—if their people have taken the time to observe exactly what each of those pooches does before the floodgates are opened.

- Begin by choosing a phrase that you can use to cue your dog that it's time to pee. Good ones include "Go potty," and "Do your business."
- Walk your dog to his potty spot during one of his regular bathroom breaks. As he begins his pre-peeing maneuvers, say the phrase you've chosen, and continue to say it as he actually does the deed.
- Repeat this process every time you take him for a pit stop. Eventually, he'll associate the phrase with the act of urinating and respond accordingly. When he does, praise him lavishly.

ASKING TO GO OUT

This skill is even more useful than peeing on command. Some dogs learn to do this themselves as part of their housetraining, but others need a little more prompting.

- Start by getting something that can hang from a doorknob within reach of your dog's nose or paw and will make a pleasant noise when he touches it; a set of sleigh bells or wind chimes (if the chimes aren't sharp) will do the job.
- Ring the chimes every time you take your dog for a potty break.
- Soon, your dog will try to examine the chimes. When he does, praise him lavishly (even if the examination is a solitary sniff), and take him outside.
- Eventually, he'll tap the chimes with his paws or nose; when he does, take him out and praise him to the skies if he goes.

GO TO YOUR PLACE

As much as you love your four-legged friend, there will be times when you don't want him underfoot. At such times, the "go to your place" command comes in very handy.

- Choose a spot, such as his crate or a floor cushion in a corner of your living room, to which your dog can retreat and still get a view of the household action.
- Attach his leash, tell him "Place" or "Go to your place" and lead him to the designated spot. Praise him and give him a treat.
- Repeat this process several times. Most dogs figure out what you want by the fifth or sixth try, if not sooner.

The questions and answers below will help you to teach your dog not only what he should do but also what he shouldn't do.

CURBING EXCESSIVE BARKING

My dog barks at anything and everything: a squirrel in the backyard, a leaf tumbling down the street, the ringing of the phone. How can I get her to shut up—at least occasionally?

Believe me, I sympathize with your problem. My canine companion, Cory, is a Shetland sheepdog—a breed that's known for being probably the barkiest in the universe. Cory barks at the same circumstances you describe, plus some others: the opening and closing of windows, people standing on chairs to reach high shelves, and the unloading of dishwashers, to name a few. Here are some tactics that work with Cory and other barky dogs:

Teach him to bark. Yes, you read that correctly. Sometimes the best way to begin to curb a canine's barking is to teach him to do so on your command, after which you can then teach him to *stop* that barking on command. Start by doing something that gets your Bowser to bark, tell him "Speak" or "Bark"—and praise him when he does just that. Repeat this process until you can just give the command, and he responds accordingly.

Your next step is to teach him to stop barking. After commanding your dog to bark, wait for a few seconds, then tell him "Quiet" or "Shhhhh" (a finger to the lips helps, too). Wait for a pause in the barking, give him a treat, and praise him. Eventually he'll learn to quiet down when you tell him to.

Make him lie down. Dogs generally don't bark if they are lying down. Consequently, if you can anticipate a situation that triggers your friend's bark-fests, have him lie down first—and tell him to stay in that position.

Get him moving. All too often, the dog who barks too much is a dog who doesn't have anything else to do. Increasing your canine companion's physical activity may tire him out enough that he'll have less interest in causing a commotion.

THE JUMPIN' JACK FLASH DOG

How can you stop a dog from jumping up on you? I didn't mind when he was a puppy, but now that he's a full-grown Lab, I'm worried that his jumping will knock me over.

Dogs who jump up on people usually are trying to get the attention of those people. The quickest way to stop such behavior is to withhold the attention the dog is seeking until the behavior stops. In other words, when your dog jumps on you, ignore him. Don't look at him or pay him any other attention. Even better, turn your back and face away from him. Once he calms down, turn back around, and give him the attention he's earned. Eventually—if you employ these tactics consistently—your dog will learn that he'll get attention when he keeps his four on the floor, rather than getting himself airborne.

THE LEASH-HATER

I can't get my dog to walk nicely with me—mainly because he hates his leash. I can put it on him, but once it's on, he sits down and won't move. What can I do?

Some dogs—especially puppies—need a little more time to feel comfortable with a collar and leash than other dogs do. Just like horses and bridles, dogs and leashes don't naturally go together; the idea of being tethered to a human being probably seems strange to both species until they get used to it.

Take a little time to let your dog become accustomed to the leash. While you're indoors or in a fenced area, attach the leash to his collar —but then, let go of the leash. Let the dog walk freely, dragging the leash behind him. When he's walking easily with the leash, proceed to the next step: picking up the leash, holding it very lightly, and letting him continue to walk while leading you around. Once he's clearly okay with that, you can begin teaching him to walk nicely while he's on the leash.

DEALING WITH THE PUSHY POOCH

My new Rottweiler lunges out the door ahead of me when I take him out, goes for his food dish before I even set it down for him, and just generally seems pushy. How do I deal with him?

In two words: very carefully.

Pushy pooches like your Rottie have decided that they, not you, are the top dogs in your household. They need to learn that their rightful place is farther down in the family hierarchy. Adjusting that status, however, can be tricky and even dangerous. That's why, when dealing with a domineering dog, it's important to proceed cautiously—and, if at all possible, with the help and guidance of an expert such as an animal behaviorist or a dog trainer. Most of those experts will tell you that the domineering dog needs to be taught that nothing in life is free. In other words, such a dog needs to earn whatever it gets. He should receive nothing from you until he does something for you first.

For example, before you give your Rottie his dinner, have him sit or lie down—and allow him to eat only when you say so. When you both approach a doorway, require him to sit and let you go through first. If he wants to play, make him perform a command for you before the play session begins. And make sure that you, not he, are the one to end a play session.

Dominant dogs who are headed down the slippery slope to real aggressiveness—for example growling if approached while eating or when playing with a toy—require the help of a professional. Look for a trainer or behaviorist who has a lot of experience with this problem and who can uncover the causes of the dog's behavior.

CHEWING UP THE SCENERY

My dog is chewing his way through my shoe wardrobe and my book collection. What can I do to stop this?

Chewing gets all too many dogs into trouble with their people. A destroyed pair of Pradas or a shredded copy of the latest Grisham best-seller can make it tough to love the canine perpetrator of such destruction. Here are three ways to cope with this very common problem:

Keep the chewer away from your stuff. When you're not home—which is when your pooch is most likely to apply his choppers to your things—confine your four-legged friend. An ex-pen or a crate can do the job.

Keep your stuff away from the chewer. If you know your canine companion has a thing for shoes, don't leave those Pradas out where he can dine on them. Be careful to not put temptation within your dog's reach.

Find an acceptable substitute. Chewing is a natural activity for many dogs. If your dog is orally inclined, find a way for him to do his jawboning without shredding your stuff. Many chewers love to play with Kong toys or Busta cubes, both of which have little openings in which tasty treats can be stuffed. The dog who ordinarily would amuse himself by feasting on your Nikes will be happy to ferret out the goodies you've placed in these toys.

THE SELECTIVELY DEAF DOG

I've taught my dog to come when he's called and stay when he's told to, but about half the time he either ignores me or gets up from his position before I tell him it's okay. What can I do to make him obey me better?

Many dogs seem to develop what their human guardians sometimes call "selective deafness." Such canines appear not to hear commands to come, sit, lie down, or perform other maneuvers—not all the time, but some of the time. Most of the time this behavior is merely frustrating. Other times, though, it's downright dangerous—such as when a dog who's bolted out the door and headed for a busy highway ignores a command to come back home. Here are some strategies for curing this aggravating pseudo-malady:

Go back to square one. If your dog obeys you only sporadically, he may need some remedial training. Reteach your dog the commands he's ignoring and reward him with treats when he complies.

Work lessons into everyday life. Training need not be limited to twice-daily sessions dedicated to the canine learner. In fact, your teaching will be more effective if you find ways to integrate those lessons into your dog's daily life. For example, try putting your dog on a down-stay while you're in the kitchen fixing dinner. Call him over to come sit with you while you're watching TV. Have him sit before he gets his daily cookie from the mailman.

Tell him only once. If your dog doesn't comply the first time you tell him to sit or lie down, don't tell him again. Repeating the command simply teaches him that he doesn't need to listen the first time around. Instead, physically guide him into position— and then praise him.

Make him want to obey. The selectively deaf dog may not want to obey because he doesn't like what happens when he does. For example, commanding a free-running dog to come so that you can leash him up may cause him to think twice the next time you call him. Instead, praise him and show some affection *before* you attach the leash.

Know his limitations. Some dogs never quite "get" a particular command or maneuver—which means that their people need to work around those failures. For example, if your dog doesn't always come when you call him, keep him on a leash or in a fenced yard when he's outside. If he won't get off the couch when you tell him to, don't let him up onto the couch in the first place.

HOW TO FIND AN OBEDIENCE CLASS

Sure, it's possible to train your dog all by yourself. A little knowledge, a little patience, and a little time are often all that's needed to teach your dog some basic canine manners.

But the process can be a lot more fun and a lot more effective if you find an obedience class for yourself and your canine companion. There, a qualified instructor can refine your teaching technique and accelerate your canine's learning curve. Spending time with other dogs and their people also builds your dog's social skills and gives you some other dog people to chat with.

Here's what to keep in mind when finding and evaluating an obedience class:

Find the right class for your dog. A dog who's older than six months of age shouldn't be going to puppy kindergarten—and a puppy shouldn't be enrolled in an obedience class for adult dogs. Check the class description carefully to make sure that the one you're considering is right for your four-legged friend.

Ask around. Your breeder, veterinarian, neighbors, and local animal shelters can all help you find the right trainer and class for your dog. Don't be afraid to talk to strangers, either: If you see a dog who's exceptionally well behaved, ask his human where they both got their training. (You'll make the human's day!)

Look for health requirements. An obedience school should require that the canine enrollees have current rabies vaccinations; classes for puppies should mandate all necessary puppy shots.

Visit a class. Before deciding upon a specific instructor or class, visit a session—but leave your dog at home. Study not only the instructor but also the students. Do they all seem happy? Do they appear to be having fun? Is the instructor gentle and cheerful? Do both the students (both human and canine) seem to like the instructor?

Think positive. Any obedience class —especially those geared to puppies—should emphasize positive reinforcement. If the class you're considering advocates the use of choke collars (sometimes called training collars) or other harsh corrections, reconsider.

CHAPTER 16

Sharing Your Life with Your New Dog

·

AS TIME PASSES, your new dog won't seem so new. The two of you will settle into a routine that will expand and deepen the bond between you. He'll become a familiar presence in your life. But the familiar can become joyful, too—in fact, more joyful than the novelty he currently brings.

However, change is inevitable. Children grow up and leave the homes they shared with their parents. Single people find mates, create new homes with them, and have children of their own. People who are married or in similarly committed relationships decide to part. Throughout our lives, we move to new homes and go on vacations. And of course, no matter where we live, life doesn't go on forever. Inevitably, we die.

Our dogs witness all these changes and upheavals, but they often aren't happy about them. That's because our canine companions are creatures of habit who thrive on knowing what's going to happen next. They're most likely to feel secure when they can count on the same things happening at the same time with the same people at the

A change in your life may have a profound effect on your dog.

same place every day. For the typical canine companion, "routine" is not a dirty word; instead, it's what gives his life meaning.

As chapters thirteen, fourteen, and fifteen showed, routine not only makes your dog happier, it makes him smarter—or, at least, makes him seem that way. For example, a consistent schedule helps a canine housetrainee learn potty protocol much faster than would be the case with a dog whose human takes a more haphazard approach to housetraining.

In fact, regular routines can help your dog to teach himself. For example, in our household, Cory has taught himself to call my daughter for dinner. Each evening, she's downstairs watching TV in our family room, while my husband and I are together in the kitchen fixing the meal. Cory watches our preparations intently—and when we start to serve the plates, he starts barking. My daughter hears him and knows it's time to come up to the dinner table.

But as much as our dogs might want things to stay the same for-ever, we humans live lives that are pushed, pulled, and otherwise buffeted by change. When that happens, our canine companions may have a hard time dealing with their (and our) altered states of affairs.

For example, some dogs react to change by acting depressed: They lose their appetites and act apathetic. Others may develop housetraining amnesia: They suddenly start having accidents in the house months or even years after having mastered their bathroom basics. Still others may react by becoming hyperactive or—in the case of a new family member being introduced—exhibiting what appears to be jealous behavior.

As you'll see in the questions and answers that follow, the strategy you use to help your own unique dog deal with change depends in part on the type of change he's trying to cope with. However, no matter what sort of altered course your four-legged friend is trying to negotiate, a few common-sense actions from you can help. They include:

Limit immediate changes. Even if your own life has changed—for example, you've moved to a new home—you should try to adhere to your canine companion's usual routine. Feed him and take him for bathroom breaks at the same times you always do. If he slept in the bedroom of your previous residence, let him continue to do so in the new domicile. The idea is to provide an island of consistency amid a sea of change.

Spend more time with him. If your life is in any degree of upheaval, your dog will be the first to pick up on it—and may feel uneasy. Reassure him that all will be well by spending a little extra time with him. Knowing that you're still there will do him good—and his loving companionship will be good for you!

But don't coddle. If your dog acts bewildered and fearful as a result of a change in his routine or surroundings, you'll be tempted to cuddle him, pet him, and otherwise lavish even more affection than usual upon him. For his sake, resist the temptation. To your pooch, such cuddling reinforces fearful and otherwise undesirable behavior long after your dog has become accustomed to his new circumstances. Instead, take him for walks, play fetch, and otherwise keep him active (and distracted from his worries).

Try for gradual changes. Sometimes you can ease your dog into upcoming alterations in his life and yours. For example, if you're about to welcome a new baby into your home, you can cuddle a doll and pretend to feed it or change its "diaper," while your dog watches.

Watch for trouble. A dog who's not eating or acts lethargic may be headed for health trouble. If your pooch exhibits such signs of depression because of changes in his life, give him a couple of days to pull out of his funk. But if your Bowser's blues continue beyond the forty-eight-hour mark, he may be physically ill—and should visit a vet.

DEALING WITH DATING

I'm single—and my new dog seems to hate every guy I go out with. How can I help her deal with my having a love life?

Dogs can be incredibly perceptive. The fact that your dog doesn't like your dates actually may be significant! When I was single, my dog Molly generally disdained all the guys I went out with until she met Stan, the man who eventually became my husband. Molly adored him. I think she fell in love with him before I did.

That said, Stan took steps to make sure that Molly would like him. Your dates can do the same, especially if you clue them in ahead of time.

When your friend comes to call, ask him to greet your dog at the same time he greets you. If he's willing to give your dog a treat—either one that he brings himself or one from your household stash, so much the better. And if the relationship progresses with you, let him groom, feed, and play with your dog so that *their* relationship progresses, too.

And finally, if your dog is accustomed to sleeping in your bedroom at night, don't evict him just because you and your new friend are spending the night together. How would you feel if you were evicted from an accustomed sleeping place because someone else was sleeping there?

AND BABY MAKES FOUR

I'm due to have a baby next month, but I'm worried about how my dog will handle our new arrival. Up till now, the dog has been our "child." Will she get jealous when our real child comes?

If you take the time to be considerate of your canine "child," she shouldn't get upset over the debut of your human child. Here's how to make a smooth transition from a family of three to a family of four:

Practice beforehand. If your canine companion isn't used to being around babies, now's a good time to show her what's in store. Buy or borrow an infant-sized doll and pretend to feed and dress it while your dog is around. Make or find an audiotape of a baby crying and play it in your dog's presence. If your pooch shows any agitation—for example, barking or growling or hyperactivity—have her sit or lie down. When she does, pet her while holding the doll and playing the tape.

Introduce the baby's scent. While you're still in the hospital, dress your new baby in a T-shirt and leave it on him for a couple of hours—enough time for the shirt to pick up the baby's scent. Then, send the shirt home with your husband or someone else, who should offer the shirt to your dog to sniff.

Plan your homecoming. When new parents cross the threshold with their new baby for the very first time, it's all too easy to forget their faithful canine companion. Plan to include your pooch in the happy homecoming by having someone else hold the baby in another room of the house while you, the new mom, greet the dog privately.

Introduce carefully. Once Mom and dog have reunited, Mom should leash the dog and bring her to meet Dad and baby. Dad should sit on the floor with the baby, who should be loosely wrapped in a blanket so that everything is covered except his eyes. Let the leashed dog sniff the baby, but be ready to pull the dog back if she starts to do anything other than sniff or lick the new arrival.

Include your dog. Dogs can't change diapers or feed babies, but they can be loving companions. Call your dog to join you when you're changing or feeding the baby; slip in some petting and pooch talk while you do.

Play it safe. No matter how trustworthy your dog seems to be, *never* let her be alone with the baby. A squalling infant can activate a dog's ancient prey drive, with tragic results. In fact, you shouldn't allow your dog and child to be together without adult supervision until the child is at least five or six years of age.

BREAKING UP IS HARD TO DO

When my live-in boyfriend and I split up, he took his dog with him and moved elsewhere, while my dog and I stayed here. Since the split, my dog has been wetting the same spot near my boyfriend's old clothes closet every day. Why is she doing this, and what can I do?

Your dog, like you, may find breaking up hard to do. She may be marking a spot she identifies with your ex in an effort to call him and his dog back—or to at least let them know that she's still there.

This particular form of marking is difficult to train out of a dog. The best thing you can do is to limit her access to that room when you're not around to supervise her. Try, too, spending extra time with her to keep her busy and active. Finally, you might consider moving to a new abode, where both you and she can get a fresh start.

SHOULD FIDO VACATION WITH ME?

I want to take my dog to the beach with me this summer, but wonder if I should. When is it a good idea to travel with a dog—and when is traveling with them not such a hot idea?

Some dogs, but not all, can be wonderful traveling companions. If your dog is very old, poorly socialized, or not in the best of health, you should probably leave her in a good boarding kennel, with a pet sitter, at your vet's, or with a trusted dog-loving friend.

If your dog appears to be a good potential traveler, take him with you—but be sure to plan beforehand. Here's a quick pre-travel checklist:

Bring the right gear. The well-equipped canine traveler wears a collar with an identification tag, license, and rabies vaccination information. His people should bring along a leash, two bowls, the dog's usual food, treats, medications, plastic bags (for picking up poop), enzymatic cleaner (in case of indoor toileting accidents), and his crate.

Make sure Fido's welcome. Although America's parks, campgrounds, hotels, and motels are getting increasingly dog-friendly, not every establishment has quite seen the light regarding the joys of canine companionship. Even if you read travel guides that indicate a particular place welcomes canine guests, confirm that policy when you call to make reservations (and do call ahead!).

Be good guests. Once you and your four-legged friend have arrived, do everything you can to give the human-dog connection a good name. Keep your pooch clean and well groomed. Don't let him bark uncontrollably, and don't leave him alone in a hotel or motel room all day. (If you must leave for a few minutes, put him in his crate.) Clean up any deposits he makes during bathroom breaks. Don't allow your dog to be anything but friendly and polite to other people and pets.

Above all, follow any rules restricting dogs' access to beaches or other areas. If dogs aren't allowed, don't go there. And if they're not allowed off leash, don't think that rule is made for everyone except you two!

WHEN FIDO CAN'T TRAVEL

I'm going to a fancy resort where my dog isn't welcome—and frankly, I don't want to take him! How can I arrange for his care while I'm gone?

The pooch who can't travel with his people still can have a great vacation of his own—if his people take the time to make special arrangements for him. For example, my family and I usually vacation in places that aren't dog-friendly. But our Sheltie, Cory, does fine without us. That's because whenever we go out of town, Cory stays with friends of ours who also have a Sheltie. Of course, we return the favor: That other Sheltie stays with us whenever her people go away.

Not everyone can make such arrangements, though. If you don't have dog-loving neighbors, friends, or relatives that you can leave your pooch with, consider the following options:

A pet sitter. A person who comes to your home twice a day to walk and feed your dog can be a viable option for the pooch who's happiest staying in her own home. If your pet sitter is the school-age youngster down the street, make sure that his parents know about the arrangement and can back him up. If you opt for a professional pet sitter, find one in your area by logging on to the National Professional Pet Sitters website at www.petsitters.org, or the Pet Sitters International site at www.petsit.org.

A boarding kennel. You can find a boarding kennel for your dog at either your veterinarian's or at a commercial facility. Either way, make sure that your dog gets some personalized attention, a kennel run of his own, and that the overall facility is clean and comfortable.

DEALING WITH DEPARTURES

Our son is going back to school next month, and we're worried about how his departure will affect the family dog. He spends most of his time with Jeff, who's also been in charge of his care. How can we help our dog make the transition to living in a home without his best buddy?

Begin now to take over some of Jeff's dog care duties, so that your dog is used to getting attention from you as well as from Jeff. Walk the dog a few times a week, play some of the games that Jeff plays with him, and have the dog sleep in your room sometimes. And when Jeff departs, try spending some extra quality time with the dog. If you take all these steps, Jeff's departure won't seem so sudden or traumatic, because the dog will already have become accustomed to spending time with you, too.

FINDING A NEW HOME FOR YOUR DOG

Sometimes, a dog simply can't remain in a particular household or with a particular person. Often, a change in the human's residence is the reason. Despite an overall increase in dog-friendliness, there are some places humans must go where dogs can't follow. Among them: certain foreign countries and many nursing homes or assisted living facilities. Sometimes, too, a dog's behavior causes problems that the humans don't know how to solve. In such cases, you may need to find a new home for the dog—whether he's yours or has lived with someone else in your family. Here are some ideas for finding a new home for yours or someone else's canine companion:

Think it through. Consider whether there is any way to keep the pooch in the home he's come to know and love. For example, if a dog's behavior is causing problems, many animal shelters offer help lines, post-adoption seminars, and low-cost training classes. But if you know there's no way the dog can stay, move on to the next step: finding a great new home for him.

Network for options. Once you've decided that a new home is in a pet's best interest, commit yourself to doing everything possible to find a good home for the animal. Ask what your local animal shelter's rehoming and adoption policies are; if the dog is a pure-bred, contact the appropriate local breed rescue group. Check, too, with your veterinarian and with fellow dog lovers, all of whom may know of a person or family that would welcome the dog.

Advertise with care. Newspaper ads can help locate potential adopters, but they need to be worded carefully. For example, the phrase "free to a good home" may draw respondents who are looking for a guard dog or a dog to use in research, rather than a family pet. A more effective ad focuses on the dog's attributes and states that there will be an adoption fee.

Go online. If local networking doesn't yield any prospects, consider going online and posting a profile at an online adoption site such as www. Petfinder.org. Such sites also offer additional tips for finding new homes for pets, including questions to ask prospective adopters.

Visit your prospects. Try to visit prospective adopters' homes—and, if possible, take your dog with you. That way, you can not only see the home environment first hand but also get an idea of how your dog and the prospective adopter might get along with each other.

Get references. Ask for and call a veterinary reference to determine how a prospective adopter's previous pets were cared for. Such references can help you choose between two potential adopters.

Rehearse the move. Try to arrange overnight sleepovers for your dog at the new home. Such "rehearsals" not only accustom the dog to the new environment but can also uncover possible problems, such as allergies among residents of the new home, before the adoption becomes final.

Make a mini-manual. To help your dog adjust more smoothly to his new home, give the new family a small journal that specifies the dog's accustomed bathroom schedule, feeding times, and special quirks (for example, the dog likes to sleep on the bed).

See your vet. Before your dog goes to his new home, have your vet give him a final checkup. Make sure all his shots are up to date, and obtain the dog's records. Give all this, plus your vet's address and phone number, to your dog's new human companion.

Give an ID. Once your dog is in his new home, he may try to escape and find his way back to yours. That's why it's a good idea to put an ID tag with the new owner's name and address on the dog before he leaves your home.

Follow up. Once your dog is in his new home, check in periodically with the new family and find out how things are going. Knowing the dog has adjusted well can help ease any lingering guilt you might have.

Afterword
Facing the Future with Your New Dog

My family and I recently celebrated our much-loved Shetland sheepdog Cory's seventh birthday. Although many experts would consider that day to be his first as a canine senior citizen, Cory acts like anything but. He still races around the house when we open the windows or unload the dishwasher, just as he did when he was a puppy. He still loves to retrieve a Frisbee whenever one of his people takes the time to toss one. And he still is amazingly persistent in trying to persuade me to take a play break with him instead of being glued to my computer —just as he did when he was our brand-new puppy.

However, my family and I didn't treat this particular birthday of Cory's as anything remarkable. We gave him a few extra cookies and some additional playtime, not to mention a few extra tummy rubs. But the fact that he reached this particular canine milestone didn't strike us as being any big deal. That's because today's dogs frequently reach healthy senior citizenhoods and, in many cases, live well into their teens.

A generation ago, such dogs might have seemed rare. None of the dogs I knew during my childhood made it past the age of twelve. One of my family's dogs, a Boston terrier named Peggy, didn't even reach her third birthday. A puppy mill dog, purchased at a time when few families knew better, Peggy spent her entire life battling one malady after another and became utterly depleted in the process. When my parents finally decided to have her put to sleep, even I—a mere nine-year-old—knew that death would be kinder to her than life had ever been.

Today, of course, most people (especially if you've read this book) know better than to purchase a dog from a puppy mill. We also have access to better nutrition, more information, and a wealth of medical advances that have helped our dogs overcome health problems that routinely felled their forebears. The happy result is that most of us can count on our canine companions living to healthy old ages.

Right now, you may not be concerned about the golden years that are in the future for your new dog. But while your new friend probably is the picture of canine vigor and energy now, he certainly isn't immortal. Sooner or later, his age will catch up with him. This final chapter helps you look ahead to your new dog's golden years: shows you how to know when he's reached them and how to help him enjoy them.

SIGNS OF AGING

Not every dog who reaches the age of seven is ready to embark on senior citizenhood. Some, like Cory, appear to have taken more than a few dips in the mythical fountain of youth. But for many dogs, size is the most important factor in dictating when age begins to show. For example, a dog who weighs less than twenty pounds may not show her age until she passes her twelfth birthday. By contrast, a dog who weighs more than ninety pounds may seem like a senior citizen at the tender age of five.

But no matter what your particular dog's age or size is, there are certain signs that he's about to join the doggie equivalent of the AARP. Here's what to watch for:

Slower gait. The aging pooch takes more time getting up, lying down, and walking than he did when he was younger. He's less likely to run after the toy or critter that he would have chased with gusto during his youth.

Dimming senses. A canine senior citizen may not hear as well as he once did, and his eyesight may be less acute as well. Many aging dogs begin to exhibit cloudiness in their eyes.

More lumps and bumps. From middle age onward, dogs acquire lumps and bumps that can make them feel like beanbags to the touch. Most of these lumps are benign accumulations of fat called lipomas—but occasionally, a lump can signify the presence of a serious condition such as cancer.

Bathroom issues. Older dogs' kidneys don't function as well as younger pooches' organs do. That diminished efficiency, together with enlarged prostate glands (in male dogs) and occasional loss of memory, can lead to incontinence.

Skin and coat changes. The aging canine's coat may get grayer, especially around the muzzle, and it may become thinner than it was in his prime. At the same time, the skin may become dryer, thicker, and darker in color. He also may be less tolerant of temperature extremes than he used to be.

Behavioral changes. The older dog may be more anxious than his younger counterpart, and may appear to experience memory loss. He's also likely to sleep more than when he was younger.

Digestive changes. As a dog ages, his digestive system may rebel at the rich food he loved earlier in life. Table scraps may wreak havoc on his tummy. The results: vomiting, flatulence, or diarrhea.

Weight gain. Both dogs and people tend to pack on the pounds as they grow older. Such weight gain occurs because of a slowdown in the body's metabolism, which means that the older individual needs to consume less food to maintain his current body weight.

But while all of the above symptoms are common signs of aging, they also may signify the onset of disease. Excessive weight gain and a thinning coat, for example, may signal hypothyroidism, a condition that occurs when the dog's thyroid gland fails to produce sufficient thyroid hormone. Incontinence may herald the onset of kidney failure.

For that reason alone, it's important to have your veterinarian give your newly minted senior canine a checkup, complete with lab work. By doing so, your vet can uncover any hidden problems your pooch might have—now or in the future.

DEALING WITH AGING

While all of the above developments are signs that your dog is getting older, they're not necessarily inevitable. Some can be postponed or even alleviated completely, allowing you to increase not only your four-legged friend's lifespan but also his quality of life. For example, if your dog's slower gait is accompanied by him whining or wincing in pain, a reluctance to climb stairs, and limping, he may well have arthritis. However, this ailment can often be controlled. Moderate exercise, weight control, and special dietary supplements can help restore your canine companion's vigor.

A dog who seems to have forgotten her bathroom basics may simply need some medical help. Older, spayed females frequently develop such potty problems, but a short course of diethylstilbestrol (DES) can put a stop to such involuntary wetting. And if your dog's apparent loss of bathroom manners is part of a larger pattern of forgetfulness and disorientation, your veterinarian may be able to prescribe a medication such as Anipryl. This product is designed specifically to deal with canine cognitive dysfunction syndrome, which sometimes is called "doggie Alzheimer's disease."

Other hallmarks of aging can't be alleviated, but they can be lived with. For example, a deaf dog does just fine if he's kept on a leash in public places and learns to respond to hand signals as well as voice commands. A blind dog who's leashed in public places and has a consistent environment at home—in other words, a dog whose people know that this is no time to start rearranging the furniture—can do equally well. The dog whose advanced arthritis keeps him from jumping onto the bed or sofa will appreciate a makeshift ramp that makes climbing easy.

But other developments that may arrive with canine senior citizenhood require the attention of an expert, such as a veterinarian. These developments are mainly diseases that become more prevalent as your dog gets older. Chief among them is cancer, which is being seen more often among companion animals, as a result of their increasing longevity. That's because the likelihood of tumor development increases with age.

But just like with people, a cancer diagnosis isn't necessarily a death sentence for a dog. Nowadays, surgery, radiation, chemotherapy, and even dietary changes can help a dog fight this disease. What's crucial to a successful outcome, however, is early detection. In addition, the type of cancer and where it's located greatly affect a dog's prognosis.

Signs of canine cancer are similar to those for human cancer: abnormal swellings that persist or grow, sores that don't heal, unexplained weight loss, appetite loss, bleeding or discharge from a body opening, offensive odor, difficulty eating or swallowing, loss of stamina, persistent lameness or stiffness, and difficulty peeing, pooping, or breathing.

Other diseases that are more common in old age are arthritis, Cushing's disease, heart problems, and dental disease.

SAYING GOOD-BYE

Unfortunately, our dogs are not immortal. The sad fact of their lives (and ours) is that we usually outlive our canine companions. For most people who live with pooches, a time comes when the person must consider life without the pooch: when one needs to contemplate easing a dog into a painless, merciful, dignified death.

How do you know when it's time to consider euthanizing a dog? The answer depends on your dog, his condition, and on you. Generally, it's wise to think about ending your dog's life if the quality of that life has deteriorated so much that he's no longer enjoying being alive.

Bidding farewell to a beloved canine companion is probably the most traumatic experience a pet guardian can face. If you've loved your animal well, there's no way that you can avoid the pain that comes with such a loss. But just because we grieve at our dogs' passings doesn't mean we should subject ourselves—or them—to unnecessary indignities.

When you and your pet have an appointment for euthanasia, you don't really want to be sitting out in the waiting room at the vet's office with a lot of other owners around. You don't want your pet to go through the nervous paroxysms he usually experiences when traveling to the vet's. And you certainly don't want to have to figure out how to pay the bill afterward, when your emotions are raw and your mind is reeling.

The good news is that you don't have to. With a little planning, you can avoid such end-of-life pet care hassles. Here's how:

Talk with your vet. When your dog has clearly reached her geriatric years—or appears to be losing the fight against a life-threatening illness—talk with your vet about end-of-life procedures. Find out, for example, if the vet is willing to euthanize your dog at home (if you're interested in that option). Ask how euthanasia is performed at the clinic and get your vet's ideas on knowing when your dog's time has come.

Bring the comforts of home. You may not want to have your dog put to sleep at home, but that doesn't mean you can't bring the comforts of home to your vet's when the time comes. When I had my sixteen-year-old dog Molly euthanized after she developed uncontrollable cancer, I brought her bed to the vet's. To this day, I'm glad that she passed away ensconced in the comfort of that well-worn sleeping cushion.

Pay in advance. Ask your veterinary clinic if you can pay the bill for the euthanasia and related procedures (e.g., cremation) before you bring your dog. Most clinics will gladly accept your payment hours or even days beforehand.

Ease your dog's stress. If your dog freaks out at the idea of going to the vet's, you might want to make this last journey a little less stressful. Many veterinarians will be willing to prescribe a mild tranquilizer that you can give your four-legged friend an hour or two before the appointment.

Go at the end of the day. If possible, try to book the very last appointment of the day for your dog's euthanasia. That way, the vet can spend time with you and your canine companion instead of having to rush off to the next client on the list.

Get special consideration. Ask your vet or veterinary receptionist if there's a separate entrance to the clinic that you and your dog can use. That way, you won't have to walk through a reception area and face a lot of strangers. And don't be afraid to ask for special consideration from other people: For example, if you have a school-aged child, make sure his teachers know about the dog's death. That way, the teacher can help your child cope with his loss—and also let you know how he's doing.

Plan a tribute. After my dog Molly died, I wrote a three-figure check to the animal shelter from which I'd adopted her sixteen years earlier. Writing that check—and the letter to the shelter explaining why I was sending it—was incredibly therapeutic. I loved the idea that my tribute to Molly would help other dogs who were walking the same path she had. You can do the same, by writing a check to a local shelter or an animal welfare organization or by volunteering time to help at a shelter, where the animals are probably not nearly as fortunate as your own dearly departed pet.

TEN WAYS TO KEEP YOUR NEW DOG HEALTHY AND HAPPY—EVEN WHEN HE'S NO LONGER NEW

Even though your new dog won't be new forever, a little extra effort on your part can help keep him as healthy and happy as the day you brought him home. Here are ten tips to help you do just that:

1 **Get him checked.** Every dog needs an annual checkup by a veterinarian, just so that you can be sure that your canine companion is as healthy as he looks. And once a dog hits seniorhood, it's a good idea to get him a geriatric workup, and to boost subsequent checkups to twice a year.

2 **Don't take chances.** When it comes to your dog's safety, it's better to be cautious than to take chances in the name of convenience or expediency. Examples of putting safety first include buckling your dog into a car seat belt; not letting him run around loose if there's no fence to keep him from darting out into the street; and puppy-proofing your house before your new dog comes home and gets into mischief.

3 **Keep him looking good.** Even a shorthaired dog needs weekly brushings and monthly shampoos to keep his coat and skin looking healthy. An added bonus to these grooming sessions is that you can check your pooch for lumps, bumps, and other abnormalities.

4 **Get him moving.** A well-behaved dog—not to mention a fit and

healthy dog—is often a tired dog. If your four-legged friend tears up the house and makes a pest of himself, he may need more exercise. Take him for a twenty-minute walk at least once a day, and play fetch, chase, or keep-away several times a week. Even better: Teach him a canine sport such as herding, Frisbee, agility, or flyball.

5 Feed him well. When it comes to doggie diets, cheaper isn't better. The best, most nutritious dog food generally is premium dog food sold at specialty stores. Don't stint on your dog's nutrition; any money you spend on good dog food is an investment in your dog's present and future good health.

6 Think positive. Training goes much more smoothly if you, the trainer, think in terms of praising your dog for doing the right thing rather than correcting him for doing the wrong thing.

7 Find him some friends. Dogs are social beings who like being with their own kind as well as with people. If you can—and if your dog enjoys the experience—take him to a dog park regularly. If dog parks aren't available, or aren't his thing, try arranging one-on-one doggie play dates for your four-legged friend.

8 Include him. Dogs live to be with their packs—which, in this case, is you and the other members of your household. Your canine companion will adore being included in whatever outings you can bring him to, from your child's soccer game to a stroll in a city plaza. And don't forget vacations.

9 When in doubt, call. If your dog has a health symptom that worries you, don't be afraid to call your vet. Any vet would prefer to tell a concerned client that there's nothing to worry about than to ask a negligent client, "Why didn't you call me sooner?"

10 Love him. When it comes to decisions about your dog, make sure that love for him is the leading reason behind your choice. Put his interests first whenever you can, and you'll up the odds that both of you will be happy.

Appendix One
A Dog Breed Primer

Trying to find just the right breed of dog for you and your lifestyle is a daunting process—particularly when you consider that there are more than 150 breeds (not counting mutts) to choose from. Fortunately, the American Kennel Club (AKC) makes the task a little bit easier.

The AKC categorizes the breeds it recognizes into seven different groups. These groups—Sporting, Working, Hound, Terrier, Toy, Non-Sporting, and Herding—are based on what the dogs in each group were originally bred to do. For example, dogs in the Herding Group were bred to direct animals or people around an area, even when they haven't been trained to do so.

The next few pages will describe each of the AKC groups and list the breeds in each group. And because the most common breed of dog is really a multibreed—the lovable mixed breed, or mutt—you'll find some ideas on how to determine a mutt's lineage and how that lineage may affect the dog's temperament.

Each of the breed groups you'll read about here are subdivided by size: small dogs weigh less than twenty pounds, medium-sized dogs range between twenty and sixty pounds, and large dogs weigh more than sixty pounds. If a breed's typical adult weight ranges between two categories—for example, the male of the breed weighs more than twenty pounds while the female weighs less—the breed is characterized as both "small" and "medium," and the gender differential is noted.

Although no size is superior to the others, size does matter when you choose the dog of your dreams. The pros and cons of each size group are important to consider. For example, the big dog may be more easygoing and a better companion for an active person than his diminutive canine counterpart. However, he needs lots more food than a little dog does, and he can be harder to handle, especially for a child. A large dog also needs more exercise than a small dog needs—and if that need isn't satisfied, he may vent his frustration by chewing up the living room rug or barking all day long.

Little dogs are easier to feed, handle, exercise, and groom (you can bathe a small pooch in the kitchen sink). They travel more easily than a big dog does; for example, the small dog can travel in the passenger cabin of an airline if he and his carrier fit under a seat. However, they're much more delicate than the big guys of dogdom are, which can make them problematic in families with small children.

Keep in mind, too, that the sizes listed below are for typical representatives of each breed; however, there are plenty of exceptions. For example, most Shetland sheepdogs weigh no more than twenty pounds —but my own Sheltie, Cory, tips the scale at thirty-five pounds. (And no, he's not overweight. He's just exceptionally large for his breed.)

With that preamble, read on—and you'll be sure to find at least a couple of breeds that might be just right for you.

SPORTING GROUP

Sporting dogs were originally bred to help their human companions hunt and retrieve game birds. Some, such as pointers, look for birds that stay on land, and freeze into position when they find such fowl. Others, such as the spaniels, specialize in finding birds that hide in bushes, shrubs, and high grasses. Still others are retrievers, bred to do exactly what their name implies. Setters are the multitalented members of this group: They can run, point, and flush.

Sporting dogs don't have to hunt to be happy. They do, however, need some sort of vigorous exercise—and plenty of it. Dogs in this group generally are sociable, good-natured, and make great companions.

Medium

American Water Spaniel	Field Spaniel
Brittany Spaniel	Irish Water Spaniel (female)
Cocker Spaniel	Sussex Spaniel
English Cocker Spaniel	Welsh Springer Spaniel
English Springer Spaniel	Wirehaired Pointing Griffon

Large

Chesapeake Bay Retriever	Gordon Setter
Clumber Spaniel	Irish Setter
Curly-Coated Retriever	Irish Water Spaniel (male)
English Setter	Labrador Retriever
Flat-Coated Retriever	Pointer
German Shorthaired Pointer	Spinone Italiano
German Wirehaired Pointer	Vizsla
Golden Retriever	Weimaraner

HOUND GROUP

Like the dogs in the Sporting Group, hounds like to hunt, but their preferred quarry extends beyond birds to include small mammals. Different hounds rely on different senses to hunt: Some, like the greyhound, depend mainly on their sight to find whatever they're pursuing; others, like the dachshund, rely on their noses. Still others are big, powerful animals that can simply run down their quarry.

The temperaments of dogs in this group vary. Those that rely on their sight to chase prey tend to be the most mild mannered, while the scent hounds tend to be a little more obstinate. The largest hounds are the most independent of the bunch—but if they're well socialized, they can become devoted canine companions.

Small

Dachshund (miniature)

Medium

Basenji	Foxhound (English)
Basset Hound	Harrier
Beagle	Petit Basset Griffon Vendeen
Dachshund (standard)	Pharaoh Hound
Foxhound (American)	Whippet

Large

Afghan Hound	Irish Wolfhound
Black and Tan Coonhound	Norwegian Elkhound
Bloodhound	Otterhound
Borzoi	Rhodesian Ridgeback
Greyhound	Saluki
Ibizan Hound	Scottish Deerhound

WORKING GROUP

The dogs in this group were bred to perform a variety of jobs for humans, including rescuing people, protecting people and property, and pulling carts or sleds. To perform such work effectively, the dogs need to be large and strong—two traits that, in the hands of the inexperienced human, can lead to trouble for pooch and person alike. Working dogs are intelligent enough to learn quickly, but some can be very strong willed and difficult to train, despite all the smarts they're born with. Good training is a must for any dog in this group.

Medium

Standard Schnauzer

Large

Akita	Greater Swiss Mountain Dog
Alaskan Malamute	Komondor
Anatolian Shepherd	Kuvasz
Bernese Mountain Dog	Mastiff
Boxer	Newfoundland
Bullmastiff	Portuguese Water Dog
Doberman Pinscher	Rottweiler
Giant Schnauzer	Saint Bernard
Great Dane	Samoyed
Great Pyrenees	Siberian Husky

TERRIER GROUP

Life with a dog in this group is never dull. A typical terrier is a lively, energetic dog with plenty of attitude. His ancestors were bred to hunt and kill vermin—and the twenty-first-century terrier often acts as though he's still eager to go one-on-one with an errant critter. Sizes range from small to large. But no matter what his physical size is, the terrier is a dog with personality plus. These feisty, independent pooches do well with experienced people who have plenty of time to spend on grooming and training—and who are determined to make sure that they, not their dogs, are the masters of their domains.

Small

Australian Terrier
Bedlington Terrier
Border Terrier
Cairn Terrier
Dandie Dinmont Terrier
Fox Terrier (smooth)
Fox Terrier (wire)
Jack Russell Terrier

Lakeland Terrier
Manchester Terrier (standard)
Miniature Schnauzer
Norfolk Terrier
Norwich Terrier
Scottish Terrier
Welsh Terrier
West Highland White Terrier

Medium

Airedale Terrier (female)
American Staffordshire Terrier
Bull Terrier
Irish Terrier
Kerry Blue Terrier

Miniature Bull Terrier
Sealyham Terrier
Skye Terrier
Soft-Coated Wheaten Terrier
Staffordshire Bull Terrier

Large

Airedale Terrier (male)
American Staffordshire terrier

TOY GROUP

The fact that the dogs in this group are, well, toy-sized, doesn't mean that they shouldn't be taken seriously. More often than might be imagined, the diminutive toy dog has a big-dog attitude: The American Kennel Club cites the barking of an angry Chihuahua as evidence of this group's frequent tough-guy stance. When they're not demonstrating their feistiness, though, toy dogs make wonderful lap warmers and cuddle objects. They're clearly great for city apartments and people with little mobility, because they can be trained to potty indoors as well as out. They're also easy to control.

However, toy dogs may be problematic for households with children under the age of six, who may not have the understanding or physical control needed to refrain from hurting these teeny-tiny dogs. Another problem with dogs in this group actually lies not with the dogs, but with their people: The small size of these littlest canines often results in a laissez-faire attitude toward training by the humans in their lives. Such apathy is a big mistake: The untrained toy dog can become just as much of a tyrant as his larger, equally unschooled counterpart.

Small

Affenpinscher

Brussels Griffon

Cavalier King Charles Spaniel

Chihuahua

Chinese Crested

English Toy Spaniel

Havanese

Italian Greyhound

Japanese Chin

Maltese

Manchester Terrier

Miniature Pinscher

Papillon

Pekingese

Pomeranian

Poodle

Pug

Shih Tzu

Silky Terrier

Yorkshire Terrier

NON-SPORTING GROUP

If the American Kennel Club were to define the term *Non-Sporting Group*, its definition might be "breeds we couldn't figure out where else to place." The breeds in this group are very diverse. Sizes range from the relatively small Boston terrier to the considerably larger chow chow. Coats range from the no-nonsense hairdo of the schipperke to the often elaborately coiffed poodle. The group is equally varied with respect to temperament: Some are relatively placid and respond well to training, while others are headstrong and need expert handling.

For this reason, it's a good idea to consult experts such as your veterinarian, dog trainers, and authors of breed-specific books to get a more complete understanding of the non-sporting breed you're considering.

Small

American Eskimo Dog

Bichon Frise

Boston Terrier

Lhasa Apso

Löwchen

Poodle (toy, miniature)

Schipperke

Shiba Inu (female)

Tibetan Spaniel

Medium

Bulldog

Chinese Shar-pei

Chow Chow

Dalmatian

Finnish Spitz

French Bulldog

Keeshond

Poodle (standard)

Shiba Inu (male)

Tibetan Terrier

Large

Chow Chow

HERDING GROUP

Although the dogs in this group vary widely in size and coat type, they all have one thing in common: the uncanny ability to control the movements of other creatures—canine and otherwise. As an example, the American Kennel Club notes that the short-legged Corgi can drive a herd of cattle to pasture. And while this ability to direct other animals' movements can be refined through training, most of the members of this group have an instinctive desire to herd any ambulatory creature: ducks, sheep, cattle, goats, and even human beings.

This special talent helps make the breeds in this group especially amenable to training—and many go on to excel in all kinds of canine jobs and sports. For example, Border collies, Australian shepherds, and Shetland sheepdogs excel in the popular canine sport of agility; Australian shepherds and Border collies also outpace other breeds in Frisbee competition. And of course, German shepherds are the dogs most frequently seen performing important jobs, such as search-and-rescue and police work.

Small

Shetland Sheepdog

Medium

Australian Cattle Dog	Canaan Dog
Australian Shepherd	Collie (female)
Bearded Collie	Polish Lowland Sheepdog
Belgian Malinois (female)	Puli
Belgian Sheepdog (female)	Welsh Corgi (Cardigan)
Border Collie	Welsh Corgi (Pembroke)

Large

Belgian Malinois (male)	Briard
Belgian Sheepdog (male)	Collie (male)
Belgian Tervuren	German Shepherd Dog
Bouvier des Flandres	Old English Sheepdog

MIXED BREEDS AND RARE BREEDS

The AKC breed groups don't cover every type of dog that has graced the lives of people. For various reasons, some exotic (as in you've probably never heard of them) breeds haven't been registered by the AKC. An example is the Podengo, one of whom starred in a movie called *Soccer Dog*—and who proved to be very adept at the game.

A group called the American Rare Breed Association (www.ar-ba.org) lists more than 160 of these not-so-common canines. Each breed is assigned to a group that corresponds somewhat to a group in the American Kennel Club; for example, both ARBA and the AKC assign certain breeds to a Herding Group. Most of these breeds are described in detail on the ARBA website.

The most common breed, of course, is a nonbreed (or, more accurately, a multiplicity of breeds): the mixed breed or mutt. These canine amalgams offer plenty of advantages to the not-so-discriminating dog lover: They're often healthier than their purebred counterparts; they're widely available at local animal shelters; and they often have more stable personalities than purebred dogs do.

What a mixed breed may lack—particularly if he's less than one year old—is predictability. An adorably fuzzy little bundle can grow up into a mixed-breed dog who's far bigger than you expected—or are prepared to deal with. For that reason, it's important to find out as much as possible about a mixed-breed puppy's ancestry before deciding whether or not he's the dog for you.

If you're considering an adult mixed-breed dog, size won't be a surprise, but knowledge of the dog's forebears is still beneficial. That's because such knowledge can help you predict what sort of temperament the dog has and how he's likely to behave. For example, a Labrador retriever–German shepherd mix stands a good chance of being relatively easygoing (thanks to his Lab ancestry), but may want to herd you and the other family members (which would be a nod to his German shepherd forebears).

When evaluating any dog, however, nothing surpasses the knowledge you will gather by spending some time with the actual dog you're considering. Such firsthand information is the best way to learn what you need to know to be confident that the dog you're falling in love with is truly the right dog for you.

Appendix Two
Sample Contracts

Here are two adoption contracts that illustrate what animal shelters and breed rescue groups require from adopters of the puppies and dogs in their care. But, while these contracts are quite typical, they're not reproducible—unless you obtain the written consent of the two organizations that allowed us to use their contracts for this book.

ADOPTION CONTRACT
Hillside SPCA Animal Shelter
Schuylkill County, Pennsylvania

Adoption Contract/Guidelines

This is our standard adoption contract that must be completed and signed by anyone wishing to adopt an animal from the Hillside SPCA. Our number one concern is for the animals and we strive to place them in good, loving homes.

Please NOTE: We DO NOT refund adoption fees—no exceptions.

Adoption Contract

All animal adoption contracts approved by the Hillside S.P.C.A., Inc. are subject to the following terms and conditions:

1. The Adopter agrees that the animal will be kept only as a domesticated house pet. This means that dogs will be kept indoors except for periods of exercise in a fenced-in yard or on a leash. Cats will be kept indoors at all times unless a screened-in porch or similar type enclosure is available.

2. The Adopter agrees to have the animal spayed or neutered by the date specified above. The Adopter further agrees to provide proper veterinary care for the animal.

3. The Adopter grants the Hillside S.P.C.A., Inc. the right to maker periodic visits to the Adopter's premises for the purpose of checking on the health and general welfare of the animal and to verify that the animal has been spayed or neutered in accordance with the terms of this agreement.

4. The Adopter represents that all family members have agreed to the adoption of the animal and that all family members will abide by the terms of this agreement. The Adopter further represents that he/she is eighteen years of age or older.

5. The Adopter represents that he/she has never been subject to legal action for cruelty to or neglect of animals. The Adopter further represents that he/she has never owned an animal which has been confiscated by any animal control or humane organization for violations of state or local animal control regulations or animal adoption agreements.

6. If the Adopter is a tenant, then Adopter agrees to provide written permission from the landlord consenting to the animal adoption.

7. If for any reason the Adopter is unable to provide care to the animal, the Adopter agrees to return the animal to the Hillside S.P.C.A., Inc. The Adopter shall not offer the animal for sale or give the animal to any third party without the prior written consent of the Hillside S.P.C.A., Inc.

8. The Adopter agrees that the Hillside S.P.C.A., Inc. shall have the right of immediate possession of the animal if, in the judgment of the Hillside S.P.C.A., Inc. the animal is receiving inadequate care, is being improperly housed or handled or has not been spayed or neutered by the specified date.

9. The Adopter agrees to pay the Hillside S.P.C.A, Inc. the sum of $300.00 as liquidated damages in the event the terms of this contract are breached; this liquidated damage value does not bar the Hillside S.P.C.A., Inc. from seeking the return of the animal by judicial process or other legal means if necessary. If legal action is instituted, the Adopter agrees to pay reasonable attorney's fees and court costs.

10. The Adopter hereby declares that he/she is aware: (a) That animals are different from human beings in their responses to human actions; (b) That the actions of animals are often unpredictable. (c) That an animal's behavior may change after it leaves the shelter and accustoms itself to a home or other different environment; and (d) That the Hillside S.P.C.A., Inc. makes no claims as to the temperament, health, or mental disposition of any animal put up for adoption.

11. The Adopter understands that there will be NO REFUNDS OF ADOPTION FEE.

12. The Adopter acknowledges that he/she has received a copy of the Hillside S.P.C.A., Inc. Animal Adoption Contract Terms.

13. The Adopter hereby accepts possession of, title to (subject to the conditions of the adoption contract), and responsibility for the animal adopted and agrees to release and discharge the Hillside S.P.C.A., Inc. forever from liability for any injury or damages to any person or property caused by the adopted animal, and from any causes of action, claims, suits, or demands whatsoever that may arise as a result of such injury or damages.

ADOPTION AGREEMENT CONTRACT
Collie Rescue of Metro Atlanta, Inc.

This agreement relates to the following Collie and adopting family:

Rescue Collie's Name:_____ Tag No:_____

Approx. Age:_____ Sex:_____ Color(s):_____ Markings:_____

Adopting Family:_____

Address:_____

Telephone Numbers:_____(home) _____(work)

COLLIE RESCUE OF METRO ATLANTA, INC. has been established to provide for the rescue and care of Collies that have been abandoned, neglected and/or abused by their previous owners. Adopting families acknowledge this purpose of providing safe, secure, affectionate and healthy environments for these Collies. In order to achieve these goals, the adopting family enters into the following agreement:

- The adopting family represents that no member of the family has ever been charged with cruelty to animals

- The adopting family will keep the rescue Collie as a pet and not tied to a dog house or on a chain.

- The adopting family will provide a fenced yard for a rescue Collie. For a rescue Sheltie, the adopting family will provide a fenced yard and/or will leash walk/exercise said dog daily.

- The rescue Collie will never be attack or guard trained or used in any aspect of dog/animal training other than obedience training.

- The rescue Collie will never be given, leased or sold to any person(s), laboratory or business.

- The adopting family will provide sufficient food, water, shelter and reasonable veterinary care, including annual shots and daily or monthly heartworm treatment (Filarbits, Interceptor or other comparable brand) to heartworm free animals.

- The rescue Collie will not be abused or treated cruelly and will not be the subject of any type of experimentation.

- The adopting family will obtain and keep a current dog license and register in their county of residence.

- The adopting family will have a 30 day trial period of adjustment during which time the dog may be returned to COLLIE RESCUE OF METRO ATLANTA, INC. If the adopting family wishes to relinquish custody of the rescue Collie after the 30 day trial period, they agree to return it to COLLIE RESCUE OF METRO ATLANTA, INC. They shall not sell or transfer ownership to any other person, business or organization.

COLLIE RESCUE OF METRO ATLANTA, INC. reserves the right to make unannounced surprise inspection visits to check on the welfare of the animal and to reclaim the dog if provisions of this Agreement have been or are being violated. If a COLLIE RESCUE OF METRO ATLANTA, INC. representative determines that any of the terms have not been or are not being met or conditions of this Agreement have not or are not being met, or that the rescue Collie is not receiving proper humane care, the adopting family agrees to surrender custody of the Collie upon demand to COLLIE RESCUE OF METRO ATLANTA, INC. Should it be necessary to litigate in connection with any dispute, the adopting family agrees to pay all court costs and attorney's fees.

COLLIE RESCUE OF METRO ATLANTA, INC. does not warrant the temperament, behavior or any genetic defects of the rescue Collie. The selection and subsequent adoption of the rescue Collie is based upon the adopter's own observations and judgment. Furthermore, COLLIE RESCUE OF METRO ATLANTA, INC. is not to be held liable for any acts of the rescue Collie while living with the adopting family.

ALL transportation and costs incurred thereof are the responsibility of the adopting family.

The adopting family, by placing their signature below, signifies their understanding of this Agreement and enters into this Agreement freely and with good will. This is a legally binding contract.

_____

Signature(s) of Adopting Family

_____

Signature for Collie Rescue Adoption   Date

COLLIE RESCUE OF METRO ATLANTA, INC.
1524 Cortez Lane, NE
Atlanta, Georgia 30319
404/633-2337
atlcollres@aol.com
www.collierescueatlanta.org

Index